FIDDLE TUNES FOR UKULELE

BY LIL' REV AND JOHN NICHOLSON

Cover photo © Deone Jahnke

To access audio, visit:
www.halleonard.com/mylibrary

Enter Code
6565-2668-2949-9770

ISBN 978-1-4584-7723-1

7777 W. Bluemound Rd. P.O. Box 13819 Milwaukee, WI 53213

In Australia Contact:
Hal Leonard Australia Pty. Ltd.
4 Lentara Court
Cheltenham, Victoria, 3192 Australia
Email: ausadmin@halleonard.com.au

Visit Hal Leonard Online at
www.halleonard.com

CONTENTS

ABOUT THE AUDIO

To access the audio examples that accompany this book, simply go to **www.halleonard.com/mylibrary** and enter the code found on page 1. The examples that include audio are marked with an icon throughout the book.

Every song in the book includes a full-band recording! Typically, the featured lead ukulele starts the song, playing the notated part throughout. A rhythm instrument joins in (ukulele or guitar), strumming the chords shown above the staff (specific chord grids are given for ukulele). To close, a fiddle enters with the song's melody on the final pass through the song.

INTRODUCTION

Hello and welcome to* Fiddle Tunes for Ukulele*!

The goal of this book is to introduce the art of playing fiddle tunes on the ukulele to a broad range of students with varying abilities. For as long as there has been old-time dance music, fiddle tunes have inspired countless generations of musicians, supplementing their repertoire with exciting instrumental pieces.

Today, this body of tunes numbers in the tens of thousands and encompasses rags, waltzes, polkas, schottisches, reels, breakdowns, airs, jigs, slip jigs, novelty numbers, stomps, hornpipes, cakewalks, two-steps, marches, quadrilles, strathspeys, and freylekhs to name a few! The ethnic traditions from which these tunes come, serve to enliven and reinforce our gifts to one another as a nation of diverse peoples. To put it another way, the Irish might ask for mulligan stew, while the Cajuns might ask for gumbo, but the melting pot that is American string-band music today takes on a huge swath of influence. Attend a Chicago barn dance or a Portland contra and you'll see what we mean!

While little has been written about the ukulele's role in old-time music (i.e., southern string band, bluegrass, and hillbilly), there has long been a rhythmic and melodic tradition of playing fiddle tunes on the ukulele, taro patch, banjo uke, tiple, and the extended family of C- and D-tuned instruments. Our goal is to help the student build upon this tradition with a solid repertoire of fiddle tunes that can provide a wealth of enjoyment for years to come.

Whether you would like to join the local bluegrass jam of parking lot pickers or you want nothing more than to pass away the hours sitting on your front porch, this book will take you there. The tunes we have chosen represent a variety of styles, keys, tempos, and traditions. Some of them are standards while others are a little less common. However, variety is the key! We have arranged the tunes in both the common C tuning (G–C–E–A) as well as the more traditional D tuning (A–D–F♯–B) for a variety of reasons which you will soon learn. You will find that the arrangements run the gamut from extremely easy, such as "Old Joe Clark" and "Boil 'Em Cabbage Down," to tunes that will be well worth the effort, such as "Leather Britches" and "Morrison's Jig." We'll explore a number of approaches to playing fiddle tunes, including clawhammer, single-string lead style, fingerstyle, and even chord melody.

When the day is done, we hope that you'll come to see these tunes as little gems, chestnuts that will take on a new life as you mold and shape them to suit your own taste and ability.

Good luck and happy picking!

—Lil' Rev & John Nicholson

Frogwater: (L-R)
Lil' Rev, Susan Nicholson, and John Nicholson

SIGNS, SYMBOLS, AND SIGNATURES

Reading Tab and Notation: It is presumed that the beginning student and even more advanced players have had some experience reading notation and/or tablature. The experience of reading music can be helpful when studying fiddle music. There is nothing more enjoyable than sitting down with a fiddle tune collection like *O'Neill's* or *The Fiddler's Fake Book* and searching for a nice tune to play. With that said, most of the old-time fiddlers learned from others in their communities through an aural process. That is what they mean when they say "playing by ear." Another common situation is learning to play these tunes at dances and/or jam sessions. Eventually, if you continue to play fiddle music, you will get to a point where learning new tunes on the spot is commonplace. This, too, is part of the folk tradition in which many great old-time fiddlers grew up.

If you don't read music or have yet to learn pieces of music by ear, we have included tablature for each piece so you can learn by listening to the accompanying audio tracks and following the tablature. *Tablature* is a graphic representation of the ukulele fretboard. Each horizontal line represents a string (G–C–E–A) and each number represents a fret. The number "0" stands for an open, unfretted string.

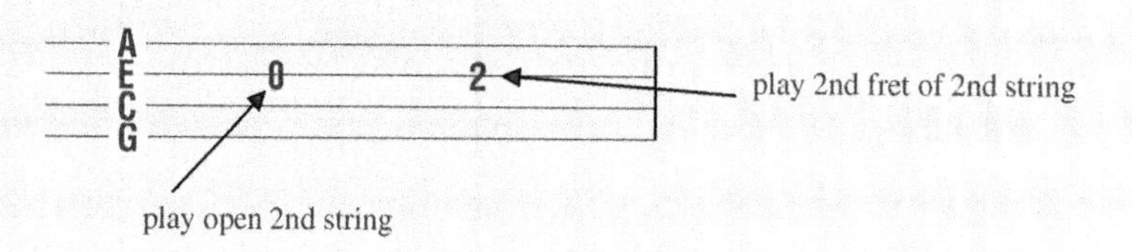

Time Signatures: The fiddle tunes in this book are played in the common *time signatures* 2/4, 4/4, 3/4, and 6/8. The time signature of a piece of music is represented by the two stacked numbers next to the clef sign at the start of a music staff. The top number tells you how many beats are in one measure and the bottom number tells you what kind of note will receive one beat ("4" = quarter note, "8" = eighth note, etc.).

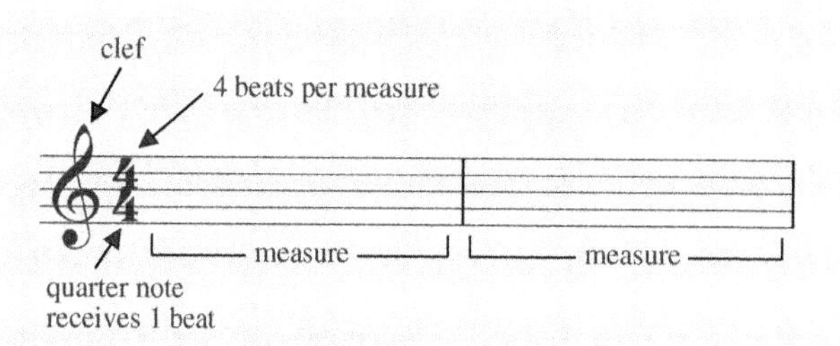

Symbols: Below are a few common symbols that will appear throughout this book which you should know.

Hammer-On: Fret the first (lower) note with one finger, then sound the higher note (on the same string) with another finger by fretting it without picking.

Pull-Off: Place both fingers on the notes to be sounded. Play the first note, and without picking, pull the finger off to sound the second (lower) note.

Legato Slide: Strike the first note and then slide the same fret-hand finger up or down the fretboard to the second note. The second note is not struck.

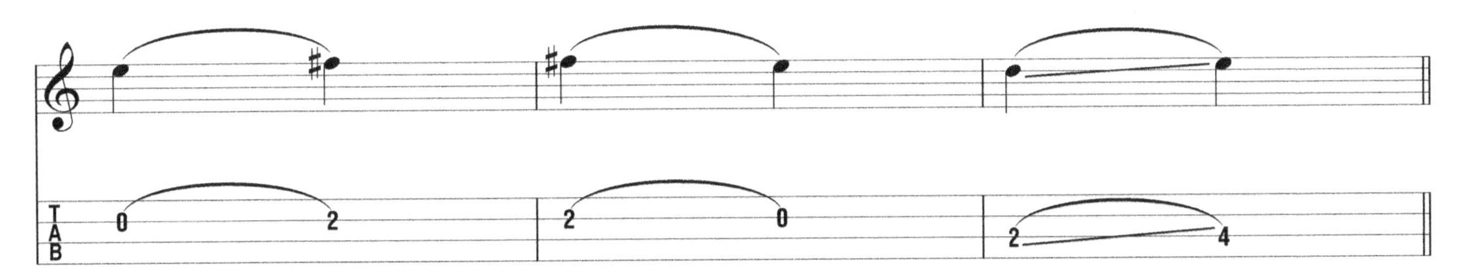

Shift Slide: Same as the legato slide, except the second note is struck.

Tremolo Picking: The note is picked continuously and as rapidly as possible.

Harmonics: Lightly touch your finger to the string directly above the fret wire without pushing down to the fretboard. Next, pluck the string with your pick hand and remove your fret-hand finger from the string, allowing the harmonic to ring out.

PLAYING TIPS

The melodies in this book can be adapted to suit any number of playing styles. However, we would like to take a moment to explain some of the most common ways in which we have arranged the fiddle tunes in this book. For example, many of the beginning arrangements for songs like "Buffalo Gals," "Old Joe Clark," "Cripple Creek," and even "The Irish Washerwoman" can all be played using what is often referred to as a *single-string lead style*.

Single-string lead style involves using the thumb and/or first finger to pick out the melody. More often than not, the thumb is doing most of the work with the first or second fingers being utilized for picking on the upbeat.

Campanella is a term used to describe the technique of playing a melody line via alternating strings. This effectively creates a ringing harp-like sound. In American bluegrass and old-time circles, melodic banjo pickers like Bill Keith often use the very same technique.

Here are some basic campanella exercises to illustrate how this approach to playing fiddle tunes might work.

Campanella-Style D Major Scale

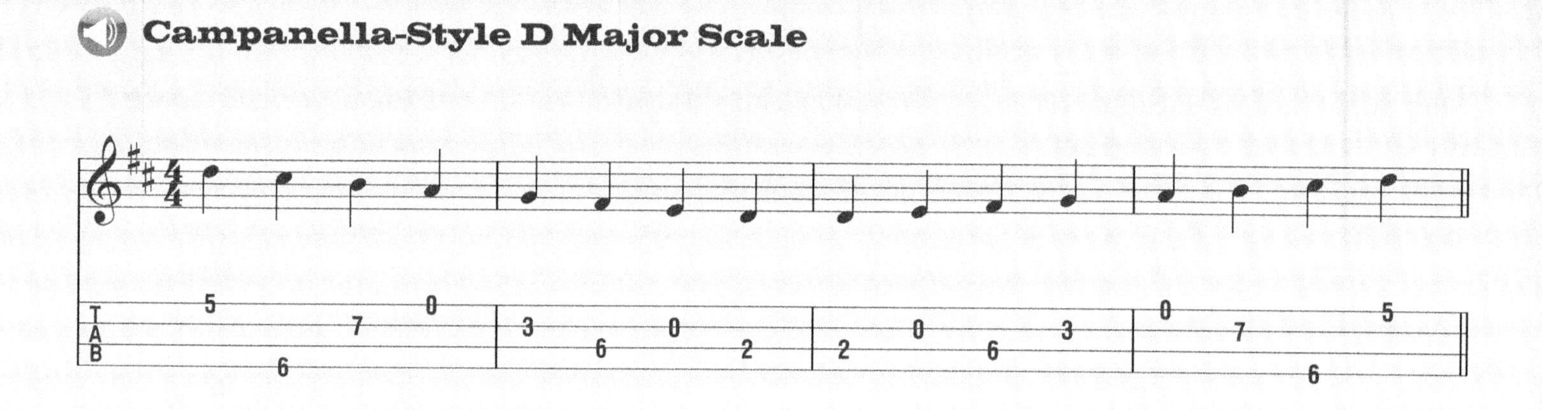

Campanella-Style C Major Scale

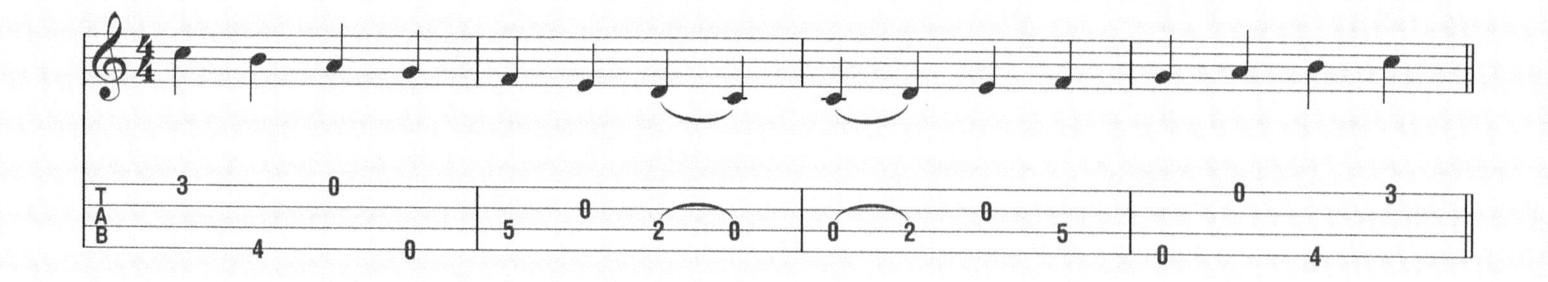

Chordal arrangements: Not to be confused with chord melody playing, chordal arrangements, like "Star of the County Down" for example, utilize a combination of rich chord inversions alongside individual melody notes to create a vibrant tapestry of color. The full sound of ringing chords, balanced with a single-string melody, create a fun way to play these tunes and make for a great solo arrangement.

Low G or high G: A lot of folks ask us if it matters whether or not they should be using a *high* G or a *low* G string on their uke. The low G can often add a rich contour and a good portion of these tunes will work just as well with either option. If you look closely though, you will see that we favored the high G when arranging these tunes. The bright quality of the high G lends itself well to playing fiddle tunes, especially when using fingerpicked campanella pieces or rich chordal arrangements, as in "Star of the County Down."

The size of your ukulele: Another important question that invariably comes up is, "Does it matter what size ukulele one uses to play fiddle tunes?" It doesn't matter. The soprano and concert ukes have a big chunky sound when strummed, and the tenors have the added advantage of giving you a longer scale length to work with. As is often the case when arranging these kinds of tunes, it is virtually impossible to squeak out a melody in first position alone. Therefore, you must reach further up the neck to find the necessary notes and/ or octaves for a given melody.

Tunings: While mainland U.S. and Hawaii seem to be happily rooted in C tuning (G–C–E–A), Canada and many parts of Europe and Asia utilize D tuning (A–D–F♯–B), which was popular at the turn of the 20th century and on through the vaudeville era. What is really important to understand here is that most fiddlers play these tunes in D, G, or A. These keys are favored because they allow the fiddler to utilize many of the open strings as well as the fingered ones. Thus, they lay down easier than in, say, B♭ or even C or F, which are naturals when using the C tuning. Therefore, some of the tunes in this book are notated in D tuning, while others are in C tuning. Throughout the book, C tuning will be assumed, while songs in D tuning will be noted with a tuning legend. If you have two ukes, try to keep one in C and one in D as you work your way through this book. When you go out to play with others, you will be glad you learned many of these tunes in the "fiddle-friendly keys." **Note:** Since D tuning is simply C tuning up one whole step, one option is to capo the 2nd fret when you're in C, instead of retuning the strings.

Remember: Most fiddlers play the tunes in this book in the standard fiddle keys of D, G, A, and C. As much as possible, we have tried to arrange the tunes in these common keys. However, to preserve the integrity of certain tunes, we chose to arrange them in keys that are simply better suited to the ukulele.

Gid Tanner and His Skillet Lickers
(Wikimedia Commons)

CLAWHAMMER EXERCISES

Clawhammer is a technique used to play the 5-string banjo. This style of banjo playing has been used symbiotically with the fiddle since its earliest inception in the U.S. Originally, this highly syncopated stroke grew out of the African-American communities down South where the banjo once reigned supreme among black songsters. Today, this stroke is used for song accompaniment as well as for playing melodies.

We'll begin by learning how to create the basic "bum ditty" sound that is the hallmark of this style. To begin:

1. Listen to the clawhammer stroke on the audio track repeatedly until you have a good sense of its rhythmic nuance.
2. Curl the fingers of your right hand into a fist-like position but not closed all the way. The thumb should be cocked outward.
3. Using the nail of either the first or second finger (either works), strike the D note (C string, 2nd fret). This is "bum" in the "bum ditty."
4. Next, brush across the entire G chord with that same finger. This is the "dit" in the "bum ditty." As your nail brushes across the G chord, your thumb will come to rest gently on the high G string and, as it does, you'll bear down on it exerting just enough pressure to push the string down and out ever so slightly. This is the "ty" in the "bum ditty."

It takes a little practice to get used to this stroke, but in time, you'll start to hear that galloping sound!

Note: i = index (or middle finger), T = thumb

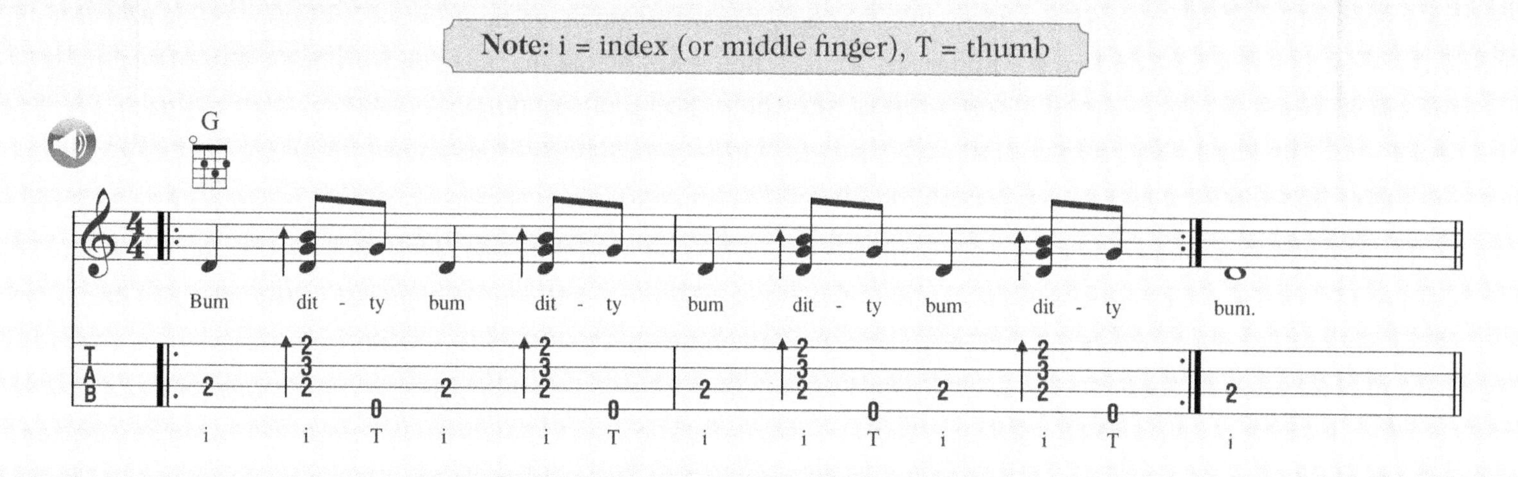

Great! Now, let's try another variation on this stroke using C and G7.

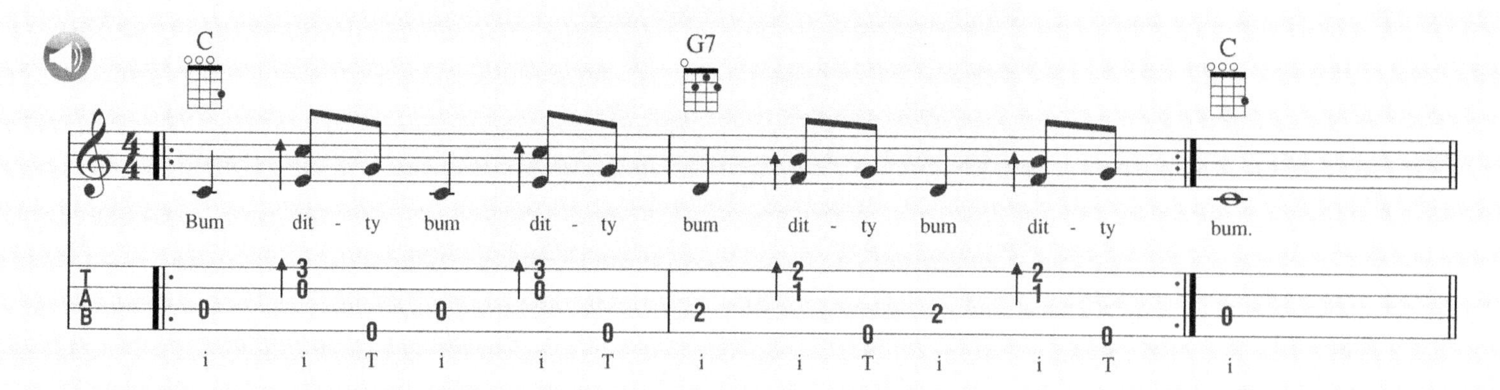

Next, we're alternating strings to get different melody notes on the first and third beats.

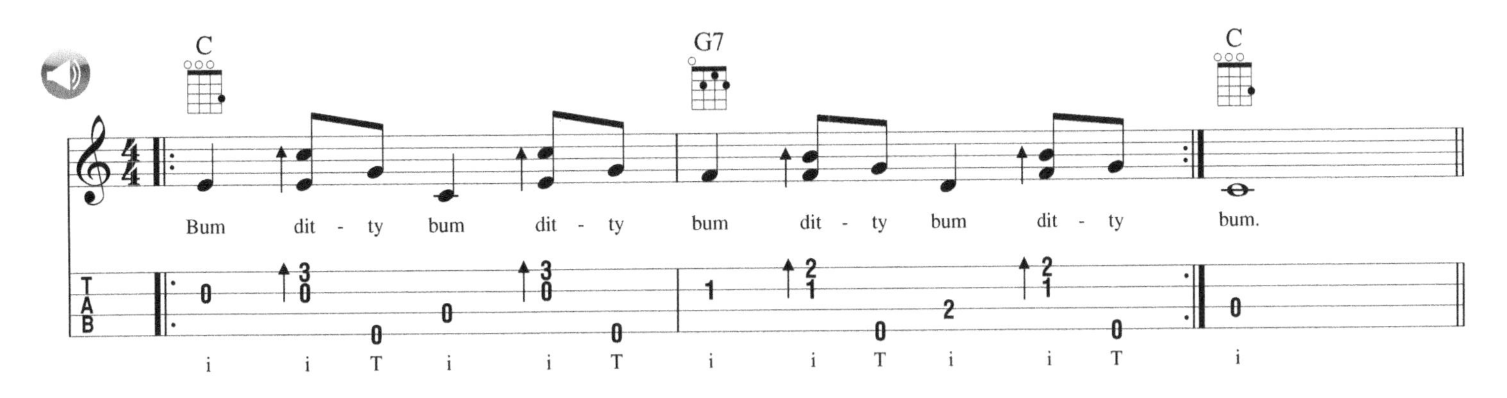

Drop thumb is an additional clawhammer technique that makes it possible to play much more melodically. The thumb drops to play strings other than the drone and picks desired upbeat melody notes. **Note:** The thumb is dropping down to pick melody notes on the 2nd string.

There are a number of great clawhammer ukulele players in the U.S. and we encourage you to seek out their recordings, live performances, and YouTube videos. Some of our favorites include Cathy Fink, the Canote Brothers, Aaron Keim, and James Hill.

Initially, the clawhammer stroke will feel odd and clumsy. But as you continue to practice, it will become more refined and eventually you'll develop a nice, solid, steady stroke!

Al Hopkins and the Hillbillies
(Photo courtesy of Southern Folklife Collection, Wilson Library, The University of North Carolina at Chapel Hill)

Mazy Todd Orchestra (Wikimedia Commons)

FIRST TUNES IN C TUNING

Boil 'Em Cabbage

Let's begin with the bluegrass standard, "Boil 'Em Cabbage." On this tune, play the downbeats with the thumb. Count the quarter notes as 1–2–3–4 in each measure, with each note representing one beat. Begin slowly and gradually build speed. This is as easy as it will ever get for fiddle tunes as most of the song is played on the A string. When you have mastered the melody, learn the high and low harmony parts. Record yourself playing the melody and try it alongside the other parts to hear how they complement each other. Also, find a friend to strum the chords and practice playing well with others.

Part 1 – Melody

Part 2 – High Harmony

This is called a *high harmony*. It will complement the melody when played alongside it or in place of it.

Part 3 – Low Harmony

This is called a *low harmony* and would sound good when played alongside a friend who is playing the melody.

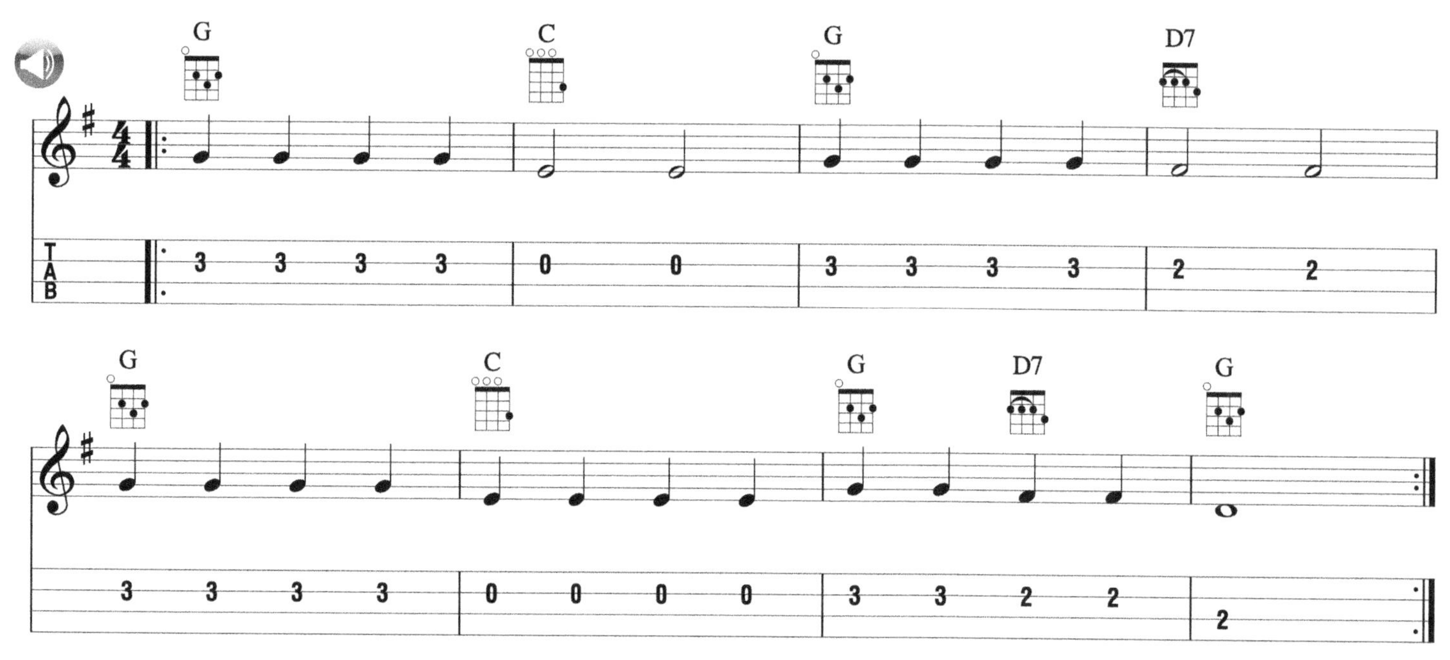

Shortenin' Bread

Start picking this one slowly, using the thumb and first finger. If you are new to playing melodies across numerous strings, then this serves as a great place to start, but take your time as you pluck across the G, E, and A strings.

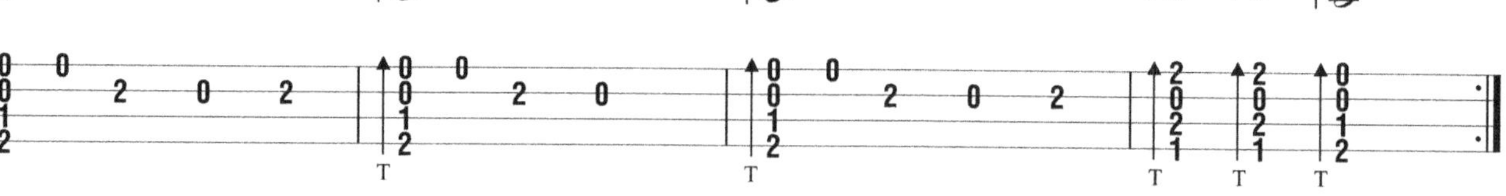

Buffalo Gals

"Buffalo Gals" is a super easy melody to play and is very common in both bluegrass and old-time music circles. We have included the lyrics here as it is often sung in addition to being played as an instrumental. Like the previous songs, play this with the single-string lead style approach, and remember to take it slow at first. Once you have it down, play it rip-roaring fast!

Much like "Old Joe Clark," "Angeline the Baker," "Arkansas Traveler," and "Soldier's Joy," "Buffalo Gals" is the sort of tune that is a festival favorite and a perennial classic. In other words, this is a "must-have melody" for your grab bag of tunes to call upon when you join a jam session with the locals. My favorite version doesn't come from a fiddler this time, but rather from guitarist extraordinaire Harvey Reid on his superb collection of timeless instrumentals called *Chestnuts*. – Lil' Rev

Old Joe Clark

"Old Joe Clark" is one of the true chestnuts of old-time string-band music. Whether you run in the bluegrass, old-time, or Nashville circles, this is one classic tune that's mandatory grist for the mill. Don't be afraid to swing it a little when you practice, since that's the way it's going to sound in a real live festival or local jam session.

Play this arrangement with the single-string lead style approach. "Old Joe Clark" is not only an important song that every aspiring old-time player must know, but it's great practice for learning how to move seamlessly between single-string melody playing and chordal work. Try keeping your fret hand rooted on the G chord in the tab throughout the A section while utilizing your pinky finger for notes outside the chord.

While Pete Seeger is best known for his brilliant contribution to the world of folk music, he has also played an important role over the years as a fine interpreter of traditional Appalachian-based music. His early work for the Library of Congress alongside his many forays into the deep South—as well as the historic field recordings made by Charles Seeger and the Lomax family—helped solidify his reverence for many of these now classic tunes. I first heard "Old Joe Clark" on Pete Seeger's *American Favorite Ballads, Vol. 5* on the Folkways label. Today, there are thousands of versions of this fine old-time dance tune. – Lil' Rev

Angeline the Baker

Stephen Foster's "Angeline the Baker" is a favorite amongst fiddlers and banjo players alike. It's a really fun tune to play. With roots in the minstrel era, it lopes along nicely and begs for variation when played at a contra or square dance. It's almost as much fun to sing as it is to play! Check out the CD *Together Again* by Michael Cooney or *Five Days Singing Vol. 2* for some stellar vocal renditions of this tune.

Play this arrangement with the single-string lead style approach, using the pick-hand thumb for the melody and for brushing the F and B♭ chords. I also like to use my fret-hand pinky to play the G note on the 3rd fret of the E string. In the B section, keep your first finger rooted on the F note (1st fret of the E string). Use your middle finger to fret the melody notes that appear on the C string throughout the A and B sections. Lastly, use you ring finger to fret melody notes that move up the neck in measures 7 and 8.

Gail Heil and Bob Bovee of Spring Grove, MN.
Bob and Gail play classic old-time music for dance and concert audiences across the U.S. They are well known for their deep love and respect for the old tunes.
(Photo courtesy of Bob Bovee)

Stephen Foster's influence on the American musical psyche is beyond mention. I doubt there is a fiddler or folk musician in the nation, as well as in many parts of the world, who doesn't know at least one of his tunes.
– John Nicholson

Cripple Creek

Makes no sense to argue about this one! Play this arrangement with the single-string lead style. The finest version of this tune comes from the legendary banjo playing of Wade Ward. Ward was from Independence, Virginia and embodied the Galax-style of clawhammer playing. Check out his recordings for County Records as well as those he made for the Library of Congress.

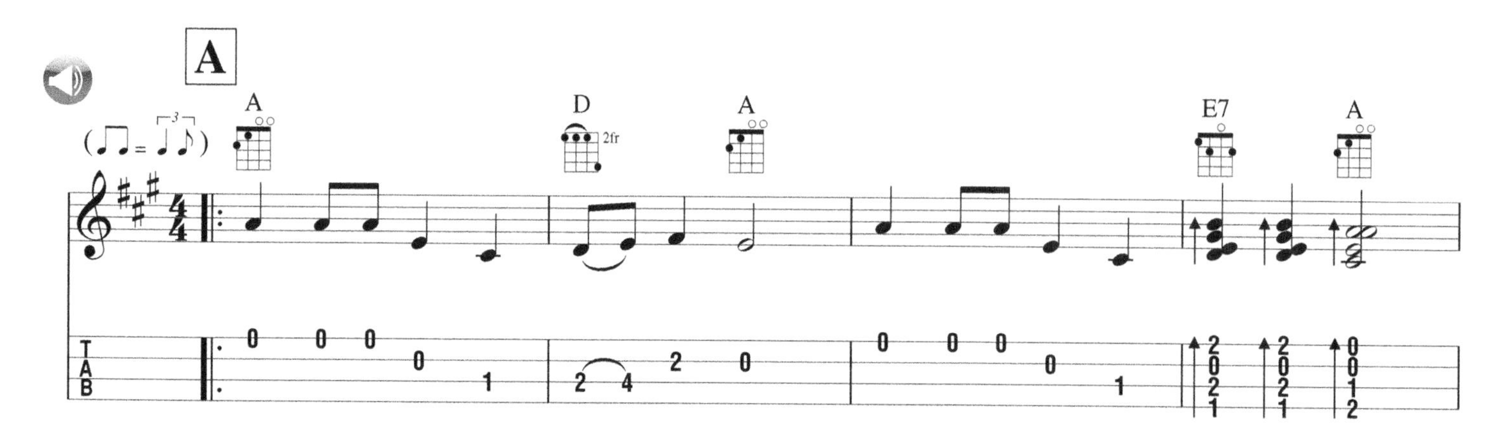

Devil's Dream

This tune is the heavyweight champion of time-honored treasures. Play it with the single-string lead style approach. Note that many of the melody notes are played on the G string; while this works really well with low G tuning, it can be accomplished with high G as well.

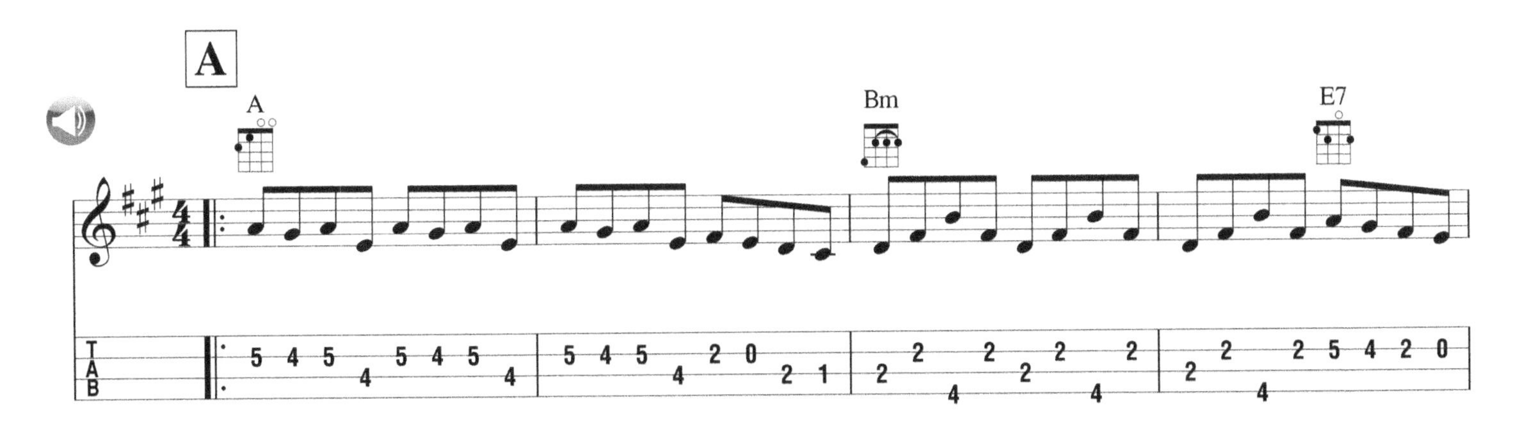

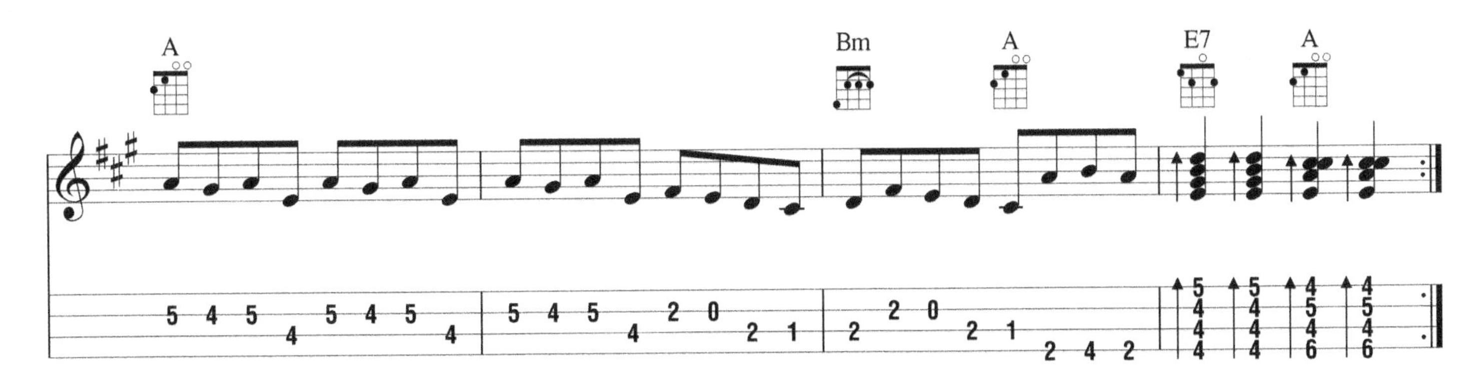

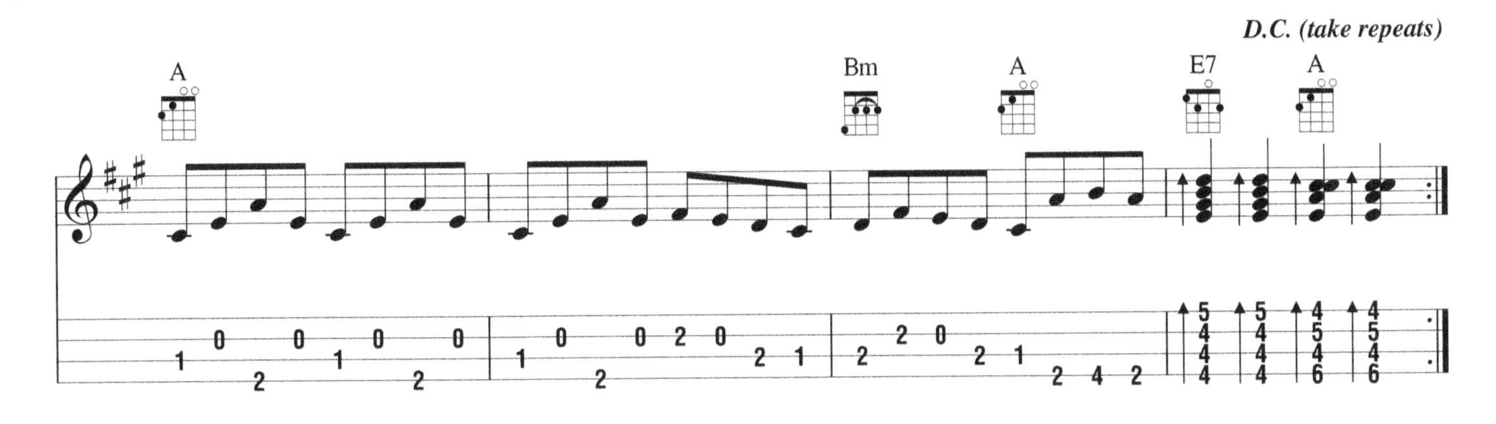

EXPLORING TUNES IN D AND C TUNING

REELS

A *reel* is a lively Celtic dance in 4/4 time with regular four-measure phrases.

Turkey in the Straw

This classic tune has spanned the generations from the minstrel stage to the ice cream truck! It also has the distinction of being the first old-time fiddle tune recorded for commercial release. It was initially recorded on June 30, 1922 as a duet by Texas fiddler Eck Robertson and Confederate Civil War veteran, Henry C. Gilliland.

This is a fingerstyle arrangement mixed with single-note melody lines and also including double-stops and chord strums. In the B part, syncopated double-stops are played off of movable chord shapes. Try to throw in the quick "Vo-do-dee-o" strum while sliding the chord form into measure 14.

Soldier's Joy

This tune dates back to the Civil War and the term "Soldier's Joy" refers to the combination of whiskey, beer, and morphine used by wounded soldiers. Here's a sample of the lyrics: "Gimme some of that Soldier's Joy, you know what I mean, I don't want to hurt no more my leg is turnin' green."

Arkansas Traveler

First published in 1847, this tune has become one of the most recorded songs in American history. The first of these recordings was done by Eck Robertson and Henry C. Gilliland on June 30th, 1922.

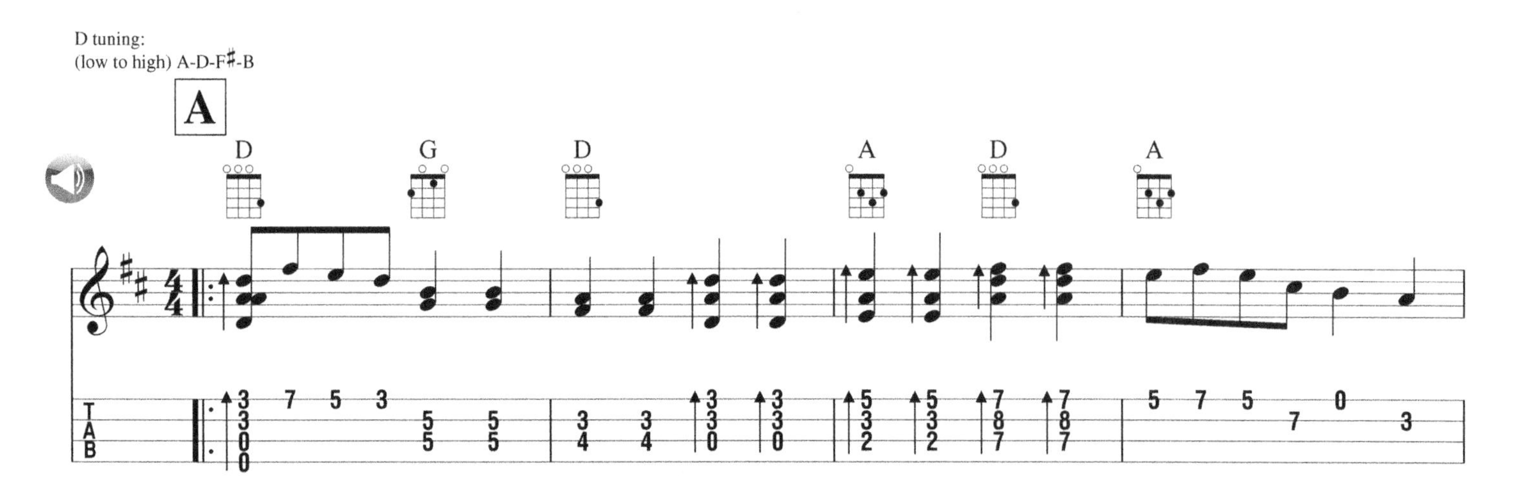

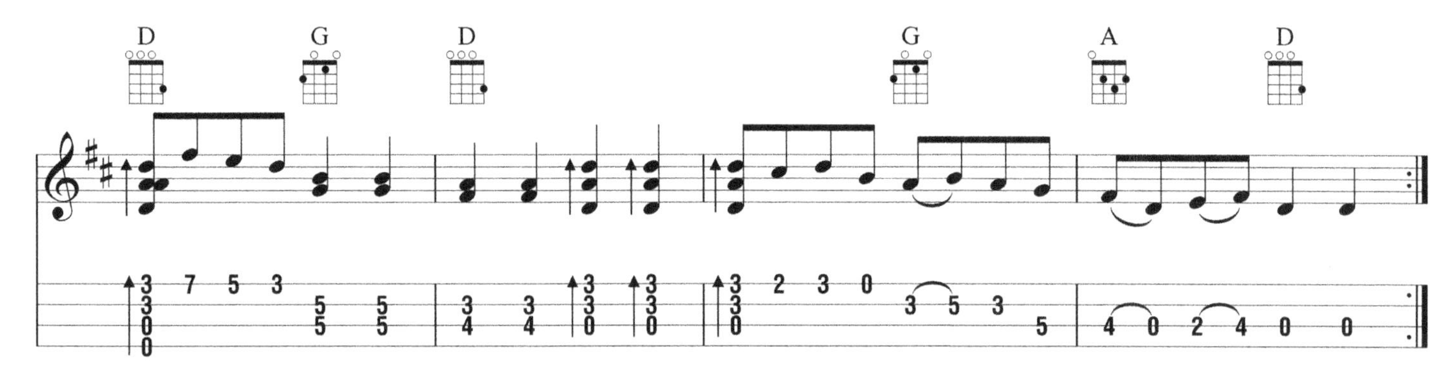

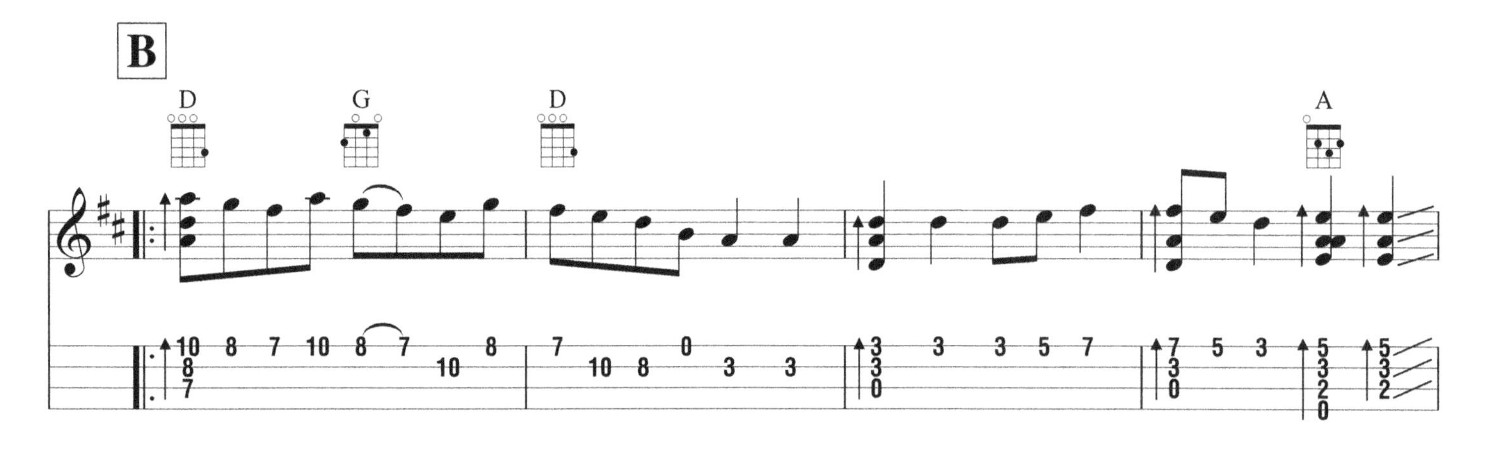

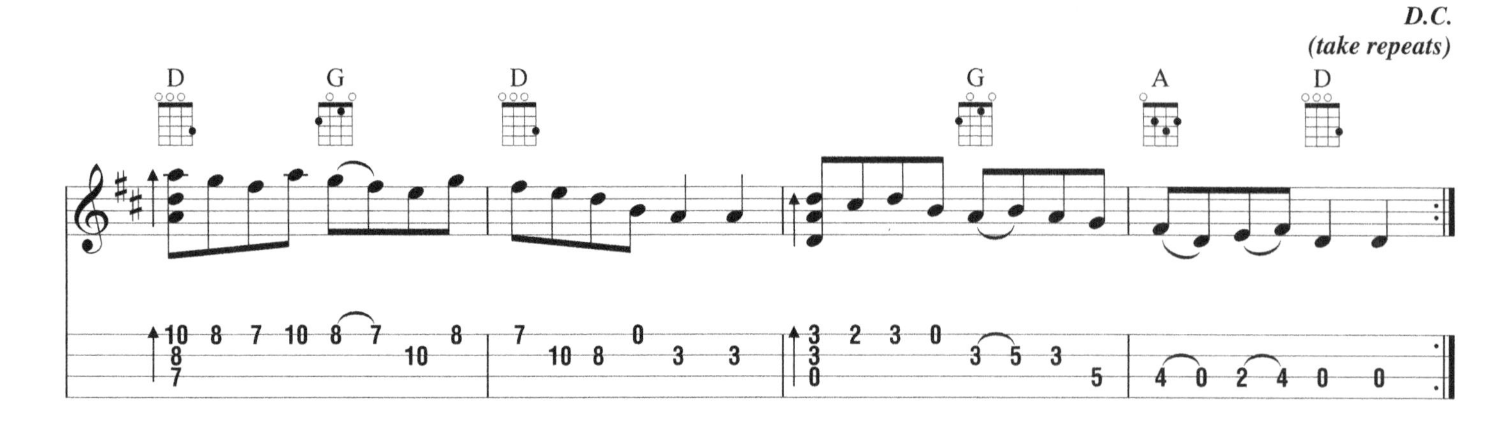

Red Haired Boy

The Gaelic translation of this title is "Goilla Rua." In Celtic, it's "Gilderoy" or "Son of the Red Haired Man." Some believe the tune was written to commemorate a real-life rogue and bandit!

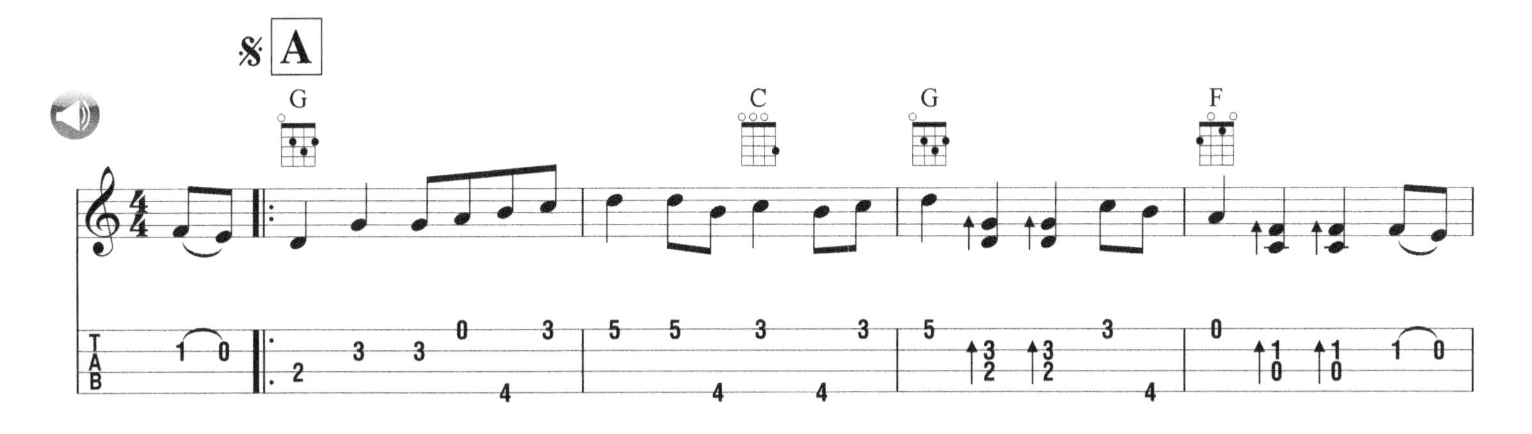

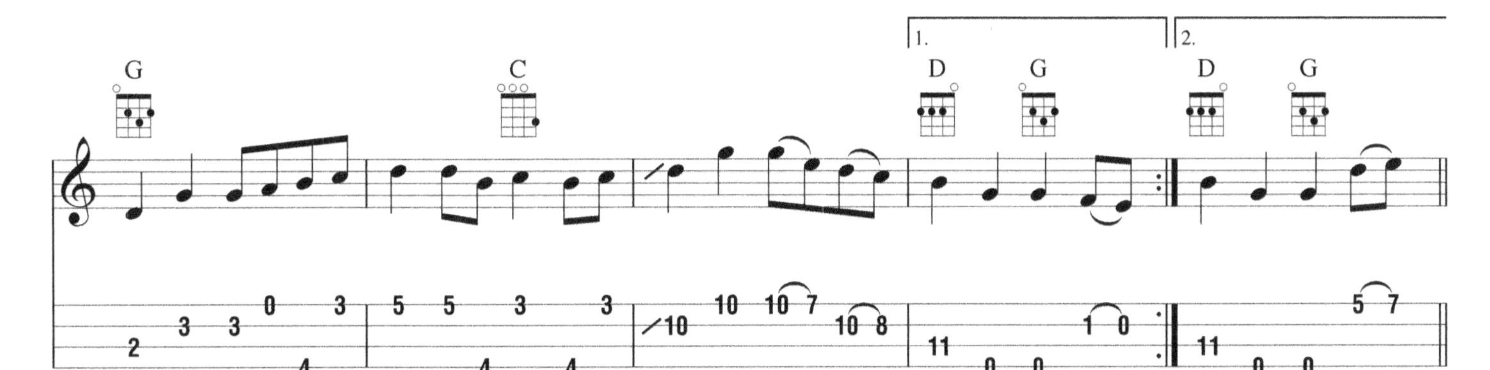

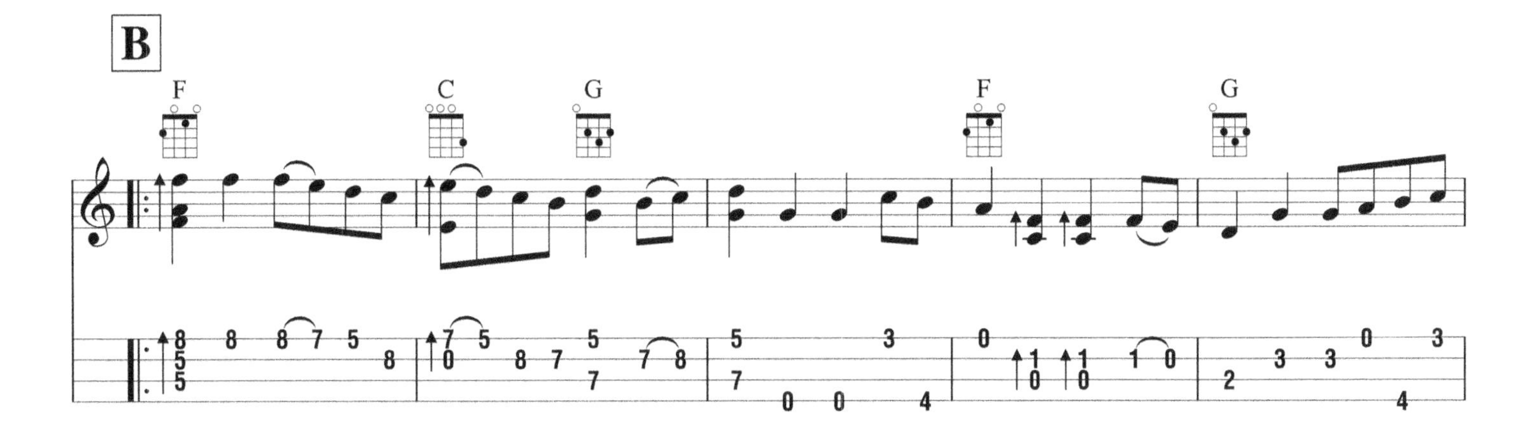

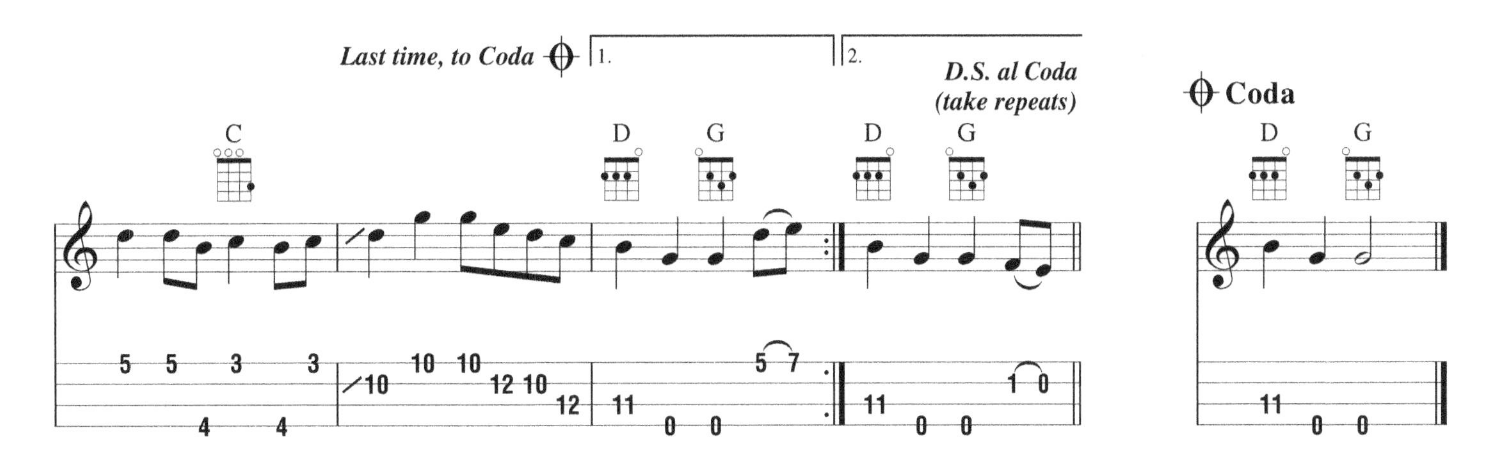

Whiskey Before Breakfast

"Whiskey Before Breakfast" is a fun and popular tune, often played at bluegrass, old-time, and even Irish sessions. This version is played mostly in the single-note style. Be sure to start the picking with your index finger in measures 2 and 6. Also, it helps to hold the double-stop shapes implied in the tab in measures 3, 7, 13, and 15 while you cross-pick the melody notes.

In the B part, the first finger of the fret hand holds down partial barres during the D and Em chords while you pick the melody lines that follow.

WALTZ

The *waltz* is a dance characterized by its 3/4 time signature.

Put Your Little Foot

Varsouvienne is essentially a waltz that originated in the mid-1800s in Warsaw, Poland. It picked up French, Spanish, and American influences both rhythmically and lyrically and became extremely popular in the U.S. and in many Scandinavian countries as a folk dance called "Put Your Little Foot."

Play this with the single-string lead style. I play this arrangement using my thumb, but one could also integrate the index or middle fingers. Remember, if you want to play this at a dance, you'll need to tune to A–D–F♯–B as most old-time musicians know this in the fiddle friendly key of D. – Lil' Rev

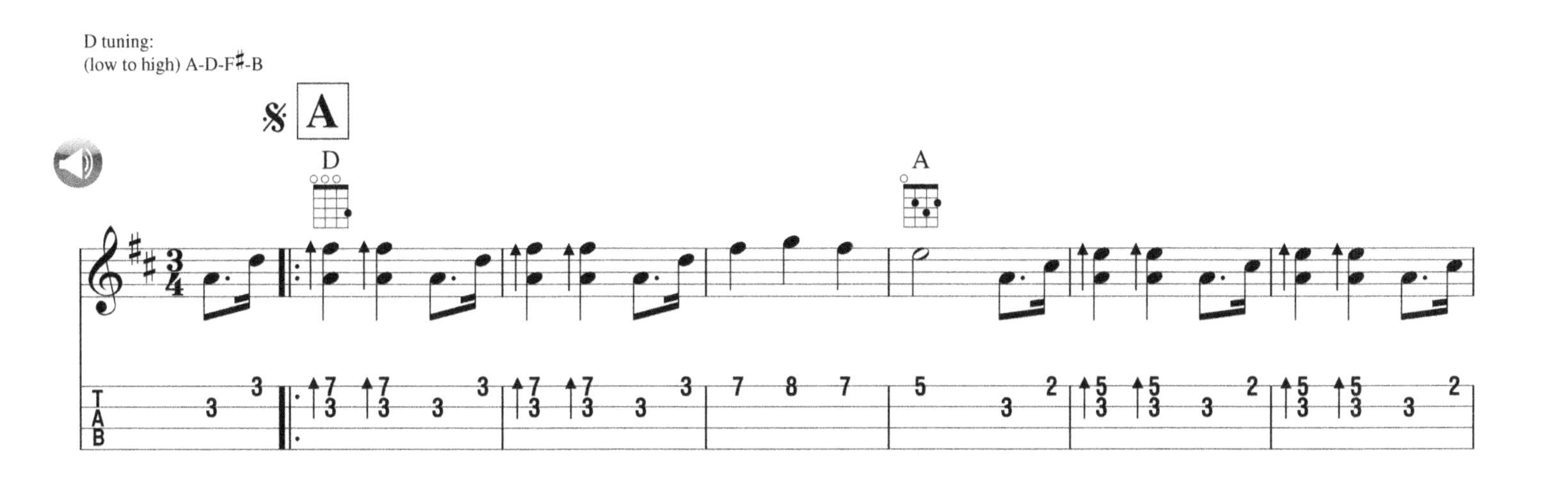

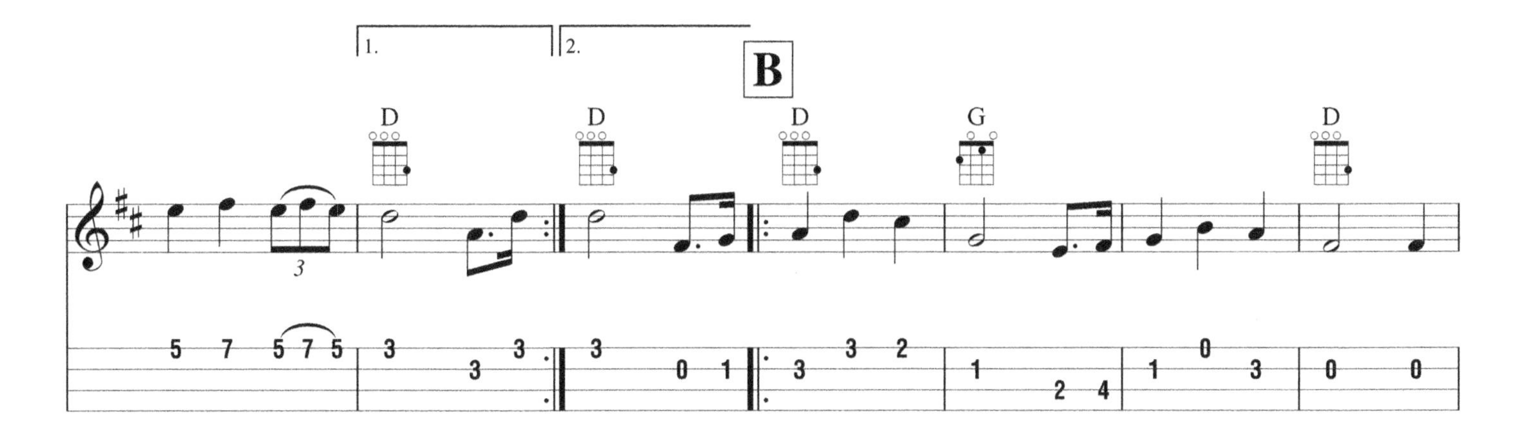

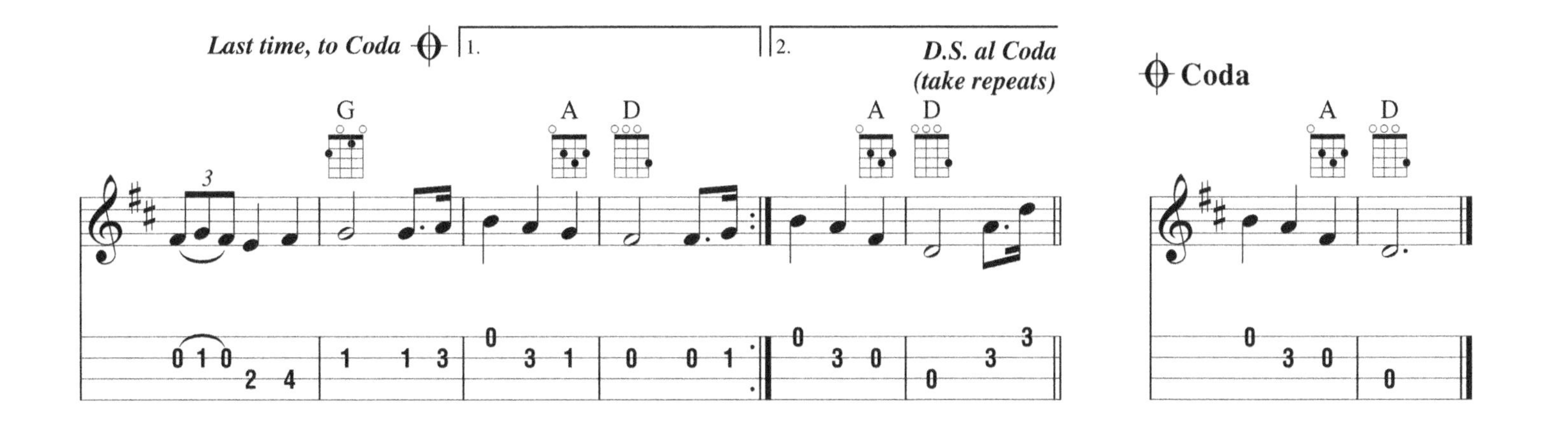

MARCH

A *march* is the music style used for marching in parades and processions. It is often written in 2/4 or cut time, as in "The Minstrel Boy."

The Minstrel Boy

1st Verse:

The minstrel boy to the war is gone,
In the ranks of death you will find him.
His father's sword he has girded on
And his wild harp slung behind him.
"Land of Song," says the warrior bard,
"Tho' all the world betray thee.
One sword, at least, thy rights shall guard,
One faithful harp shall praise thee."

This romantic poem was penned by Thomas Moore (1779–1852), who combined his writing with an old Irish melody, "The Moreen." The original poem is two verses and is believed to have been written in remembrance of fellow students at Trinity College in Dublin, who fought (and were killed) in the Irish Rebellion of 1798.

The song and tune was very popular and became a standard for the Irish who fought in the American Civil War. A third verse was added by an unknown author, which is a plea to mankind for peace and harmony. The tune became even more popular after World War I and is associated with fire and police departments in U.S. cities with great representation of Irish-Americans—notably New York, Boston, and Chicago. The melody is often played at funerals for officers who've been killed in service, typically on bagpipes.

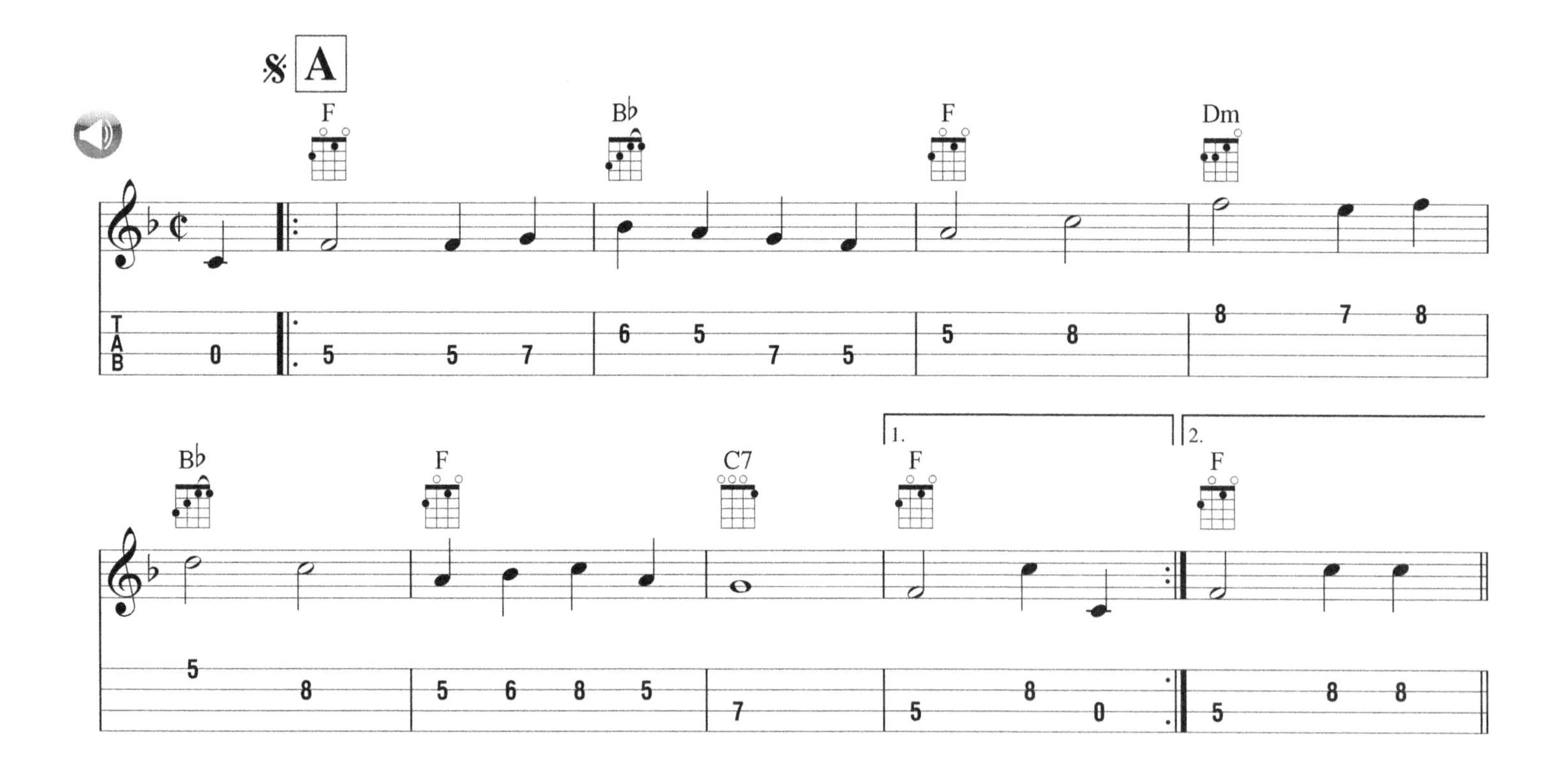

Susan and John Nicholson performing at a school show.

NOVELTY, BLUES, AND RAGS

There is a rich tradition of novelty, blues, and ragtime styles intertwined with string bands and the ukulele. *Novelty songs* have humorous lyrics or music, while the *blues* is a far-reaching style rooted in African-American spirituals. *Ragtime* is the earliest form of jazz music, with its "ragged" syncopated rhythms. Let's explore some of these great tunes.

Photo by T. Taft

Fiddling the Blues in Santa Cruz

I included "Fiddling the Blues in Santa Cruz" in this collection because there is a great tradition of blues-influenced fiddle playing. From down-home folks like Walter Vinson and Lonnie Chatman of the Mississippi Sheiks, to red-hot players like Arthur Smith, Kenny Baker, and Benny Thomasson, as well as modern-day fiddlers like Kerry Blech and Greg Canote, there are hundreds of great tunes out there to learn from if you enjoy this style of playing. This particular tune was inspired by Milton Brown and Bob Wills of the Western swing tradition of fiddling, and is played with a blues shuffle feel. It makes for a nice introduction to blues-influenced fiddle styles as they might sound on the ukulele. Play it in the single-string lead style. Try it straight first, and then really let it swing! – Lil' Rev

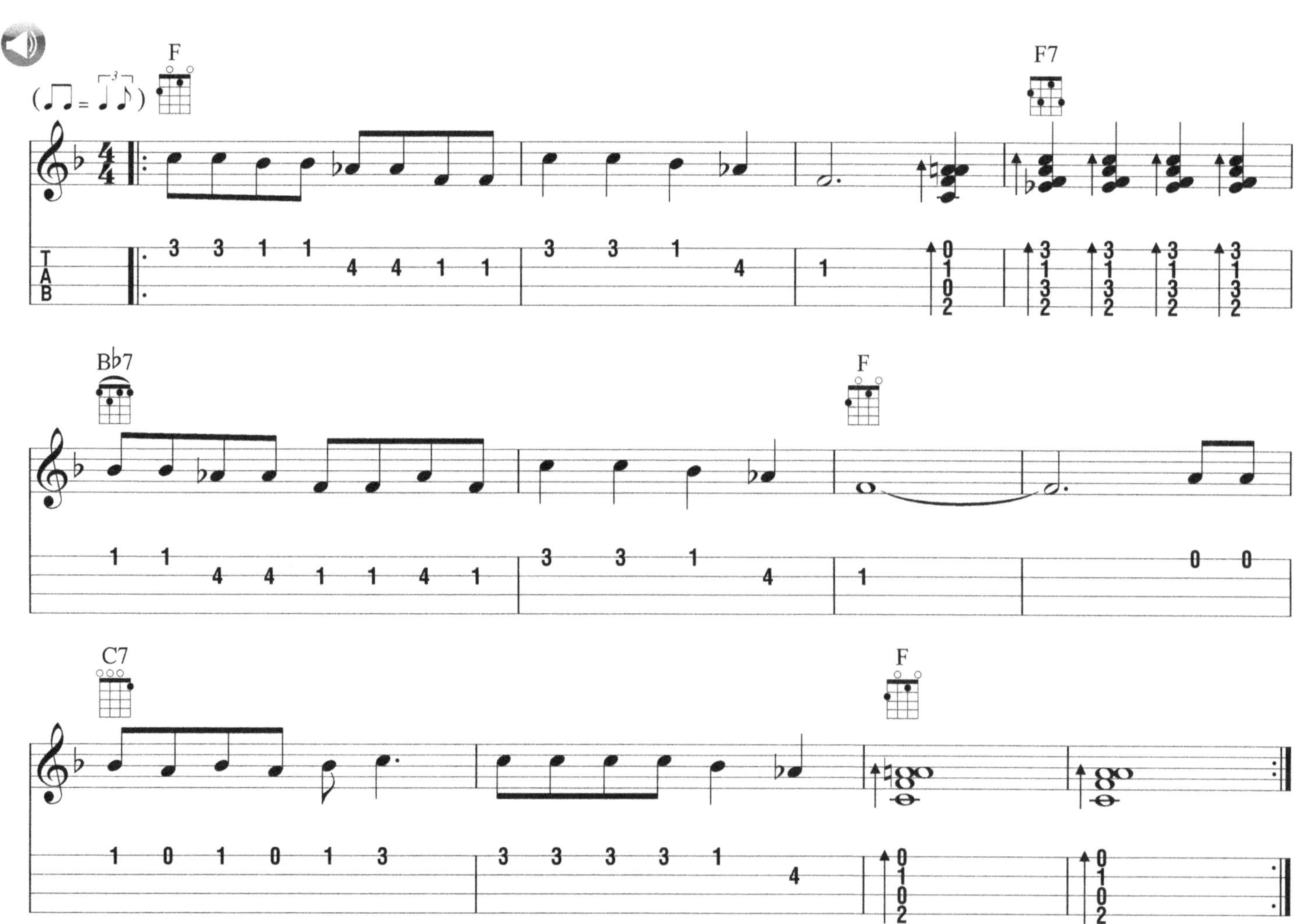

Delta Fiddle Blues

Here is a 12-bar blues inspired by the fiddle style of Son Sims. It should have a slow and steady feel, interspersing downbeat strums between the syncopated melody riffs. There is also a tremolo strum used to punctuate the end of each phrase on the barred F chord. This emulates a tremolo bowing technique, common to Delta fiddlers.

Henry "Son" Sims (August 22, 1890 – December 23, 1958) was an American Delta blues fiddler and songwriter. He is known for playing with both Charlie Patton and a young Muddy Waters.

Cakewalk

This ragtime piece comes from the vast repertoire of Bill Driver (December 8, 1881 – December 6, 1986). Bill played many wonderful tunes that were not widely known outside of the area where he lived in Miller County, Missouri.

The fingerstyle arrangement of this tune uses many techniques throughout, including arpeggios, single-note runs (even on the 4th string), double-stops, and flashes of campanella. This is a challenging tune, but a lot of fun once you get it going!

Port One Step

Here is another Missouri tune in C. This, along with the previous tune ("Cakewalk"), was documented by R.P. Christeson in *The Old-Time Fiddler's Repertory*. It is said that this tune comes down from the playing of Bill Katon (1865–1934), another legendary African-American fiddler who hailed from Callaway County, Missouri.

Also played fingerstyle, "Port One Step" uses many of the same concepts as the previous tune, with the addition of an alternating thumb arpeggio in measures 10, 12, and 14, and some arpeggiated 12th-fret harmonics. To play these harmonics, lay your 3rd finger (like a barre) directly over the 12th fret, just lightly touching the strings, while you are picking. Let 'em ring! This is a not an easy piece, but is well worth learning!

Note: The diamond-shaped noteheads in this tune indicate they should be played as harmonics.

Chicken Reel

Written in 1910 by Joseph M. Daly as a novelty song, this tune was quickly adopted by the folk music and square dance traditions. It is also mentioned more than once in classic American literature:

> "They dance all night and play a Chicken Reel."
> – *The Grapes of Wrath*, John Steinbeck

This is a fingerstyle arrangement that also includes rhythmic chord melody, double-stops, and single-note picking.

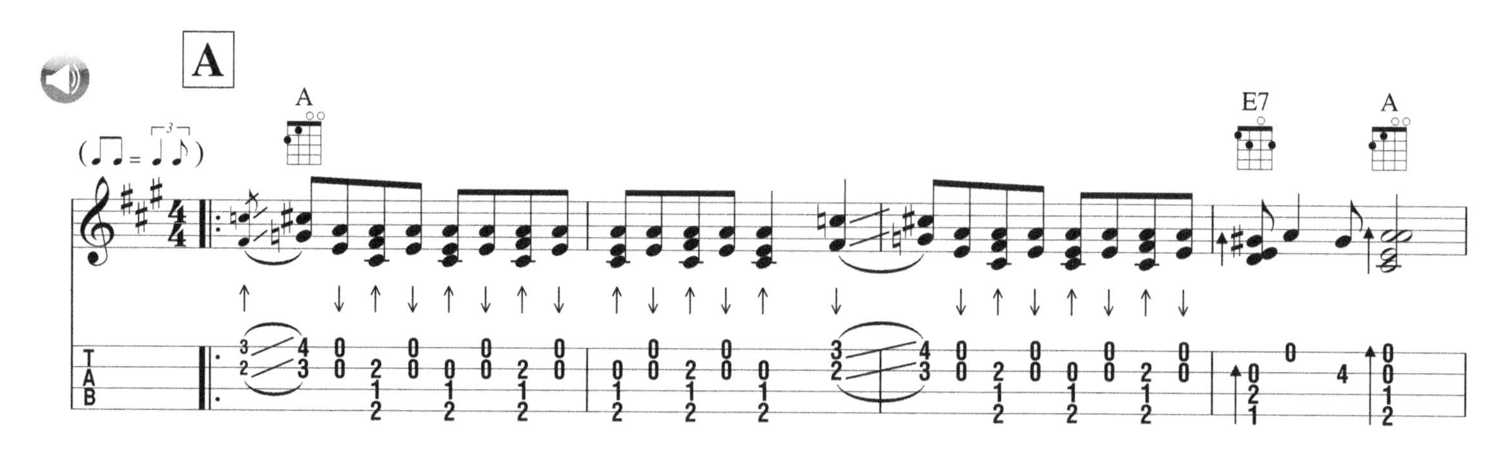

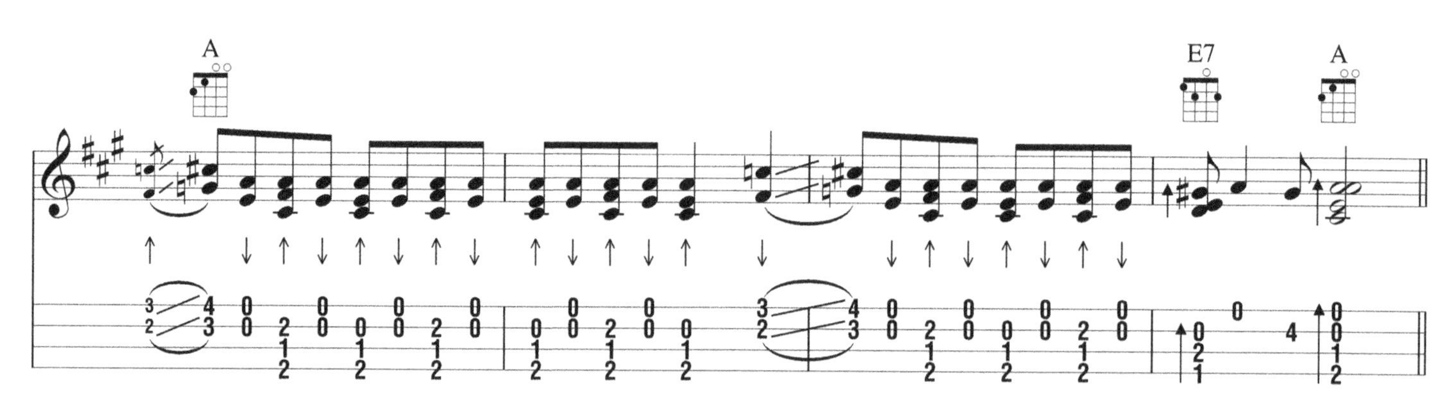

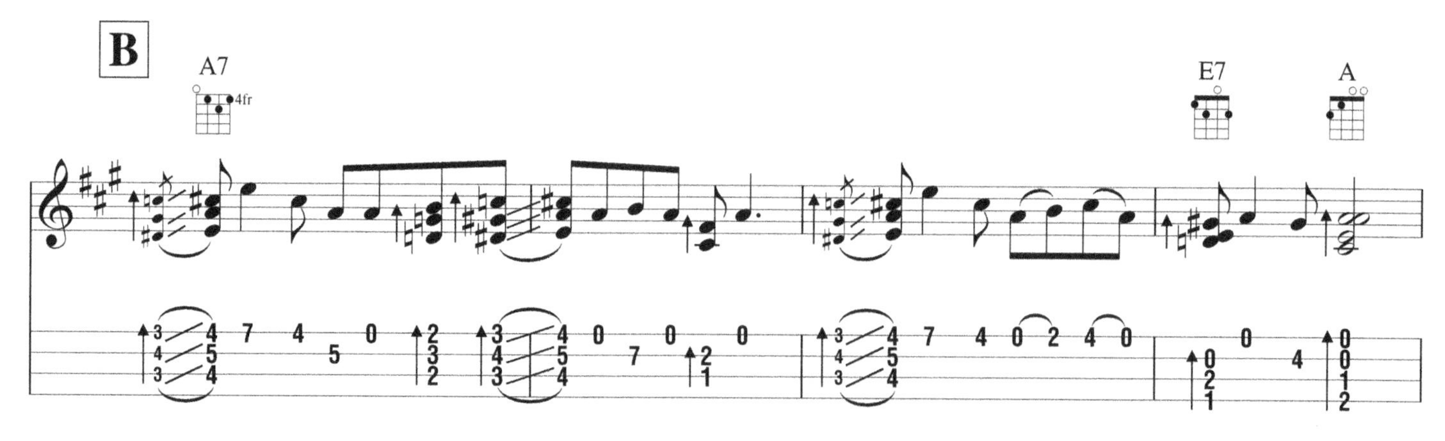

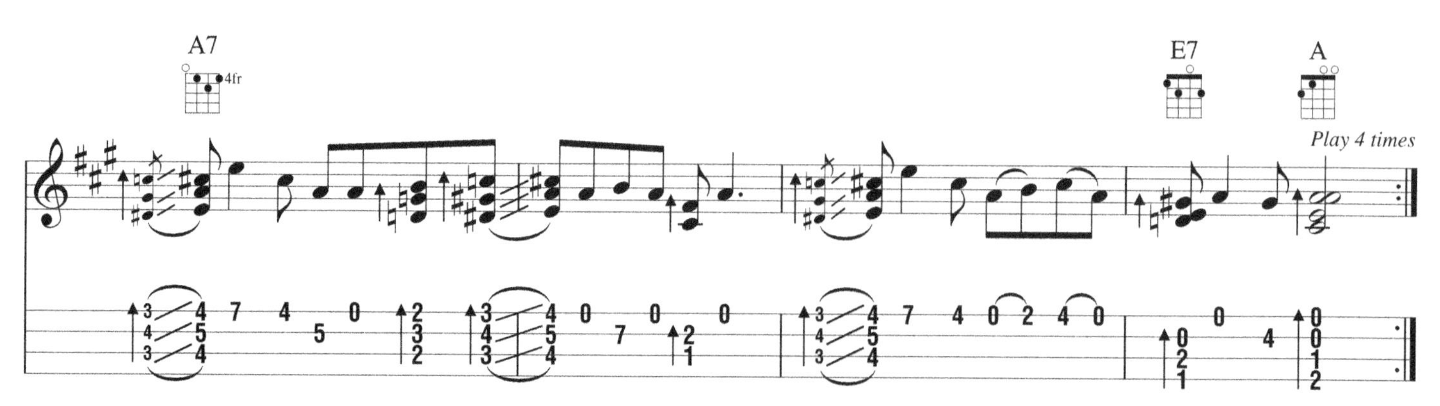

SCHOTTISCHE

A *schottische* is often thought of as a slower polka and was first popularized in the Victorian era amidst the Bohemian folk dance craze that swept throughout most of Eastern Europe and the United States.

Lumberjack Schottische

This catchy little tune comes from the Upper Peninsula of Michigan where the accordion, harmonica, and fiddle still hold sway at the local VFW halls. The music of Sweden, Denmark, and Finland are also still very much alive among its descendants. The structure of this tune is not unlike other fiddle tunes in that it has an AABB form. Play it slowly at first and then gradually let it pick up speed, but not so much that it loses its elegance on the dance floor!

I play this tune with a single-string lead style approach. In the B section, as I move quickly between chords and individual melody notes, I use a combination of my pick-hand's first finger and thumb. The first finger and thumb both brush the chords while the first finger also plucks out the individual melody notes.

– Lil' Rev

JIGS

A *jig* is a lively folk dance, usually in 6/8 time, with origins in Great Britain, Scotland, and Ireland.

Pop! Goes the Weasel

"Pop! Goes the Weasel" is often thought to be a Virginia tune in America. However, publications dating back to the 1580s from the British Library describe "Pop! Goes the Weasel" as "an old English dance" that was often performed at Her Majesties' and nobilities' balls. My favorite old-time recording of this tune comes from *Kessinger Brothers (Clark & Lucas) Vol. 3 (1929–30)* on the Document label.

I play this tune with a single-string lead style approach. Be careful in the B section, as it moves up the neck and is played almost entirely on one string; it does require some repetition before it'll lie down smoothly under the fingers. As with most fiddle tunes, it takes a commitment of repeating passages and phrases over and over until there is some perfection that has taken place. – Lil' Rev

Cream City Jig

I wrote "Cream City Jig" back in the mid-1990s for my *Uke-Town* CD. Back in those days no one was even remotely interested in strumming on the ukulele let alone playing a jig! As the years progressed and more and more people became interested, I was often asked how one could begin playing Irish music on the ukulele. I knew that "Cream City Jig" would be an awesome introduction for the beginning student. In doing so, one learns to move seamlessly between single-note melody playing and chord work. However, the melody is also interesting enough that more advanced players may opt to embellish it a bit. Erin, go strum! – Lil' Rev

Irish Washerwoman

The Scottish/Irish influence on early American-Appalachian repertoire cannot be overstated. I first heard this played by Milwaukee's finest Irish fiddler, Susan Nicholson. Use a single-string lead approach. – Lil' Rev

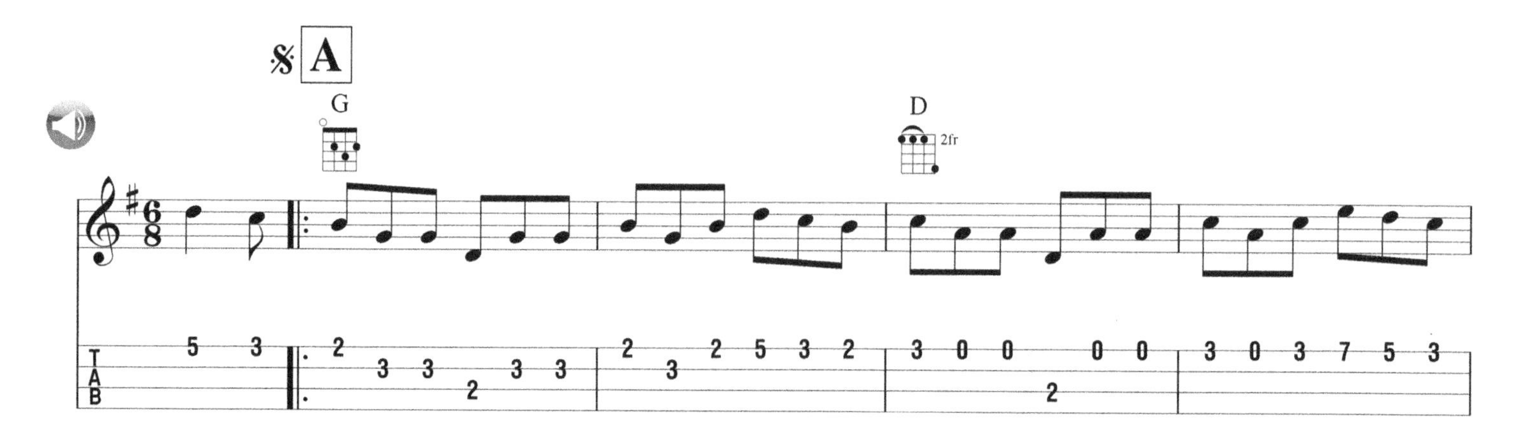

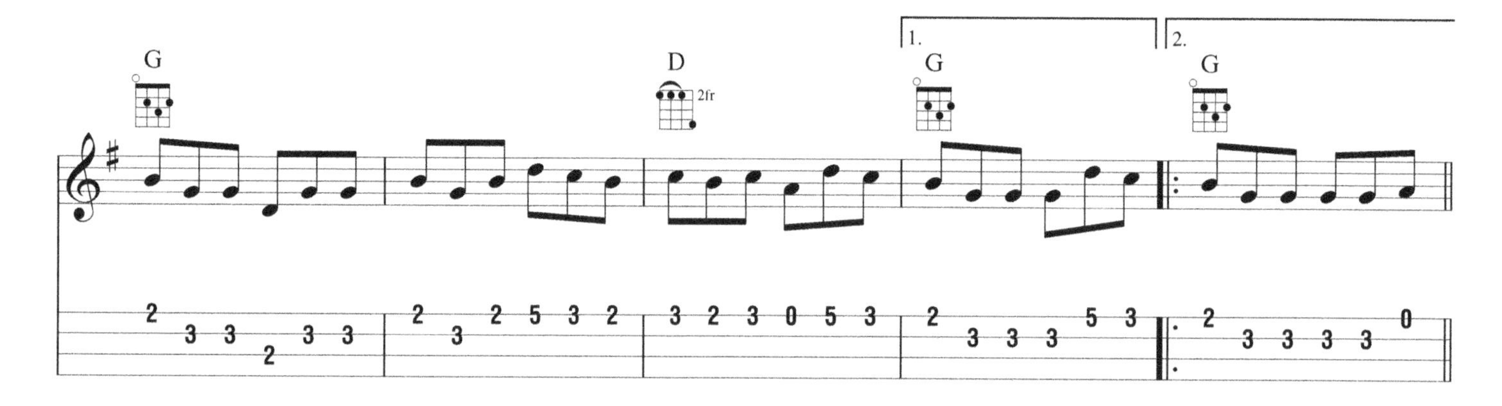

Swallow Tail Jig

As with any jig, tempo is king. So start slow and gradually build up speed as you become more familiar with this catchy little tune. I like to use my thumb to pick the melody notes on this one, in the single-string style.

"Swallow Tail Jig" is a traditional Irish jig that has been around for so long almost everyone who plays Celtic music knows this tune. Its roots go all the way back to the Renaissance. It's a ton of fun to play and you'll need it in your back pocket if you're going to attend Irish sessions at your local pub or festival.

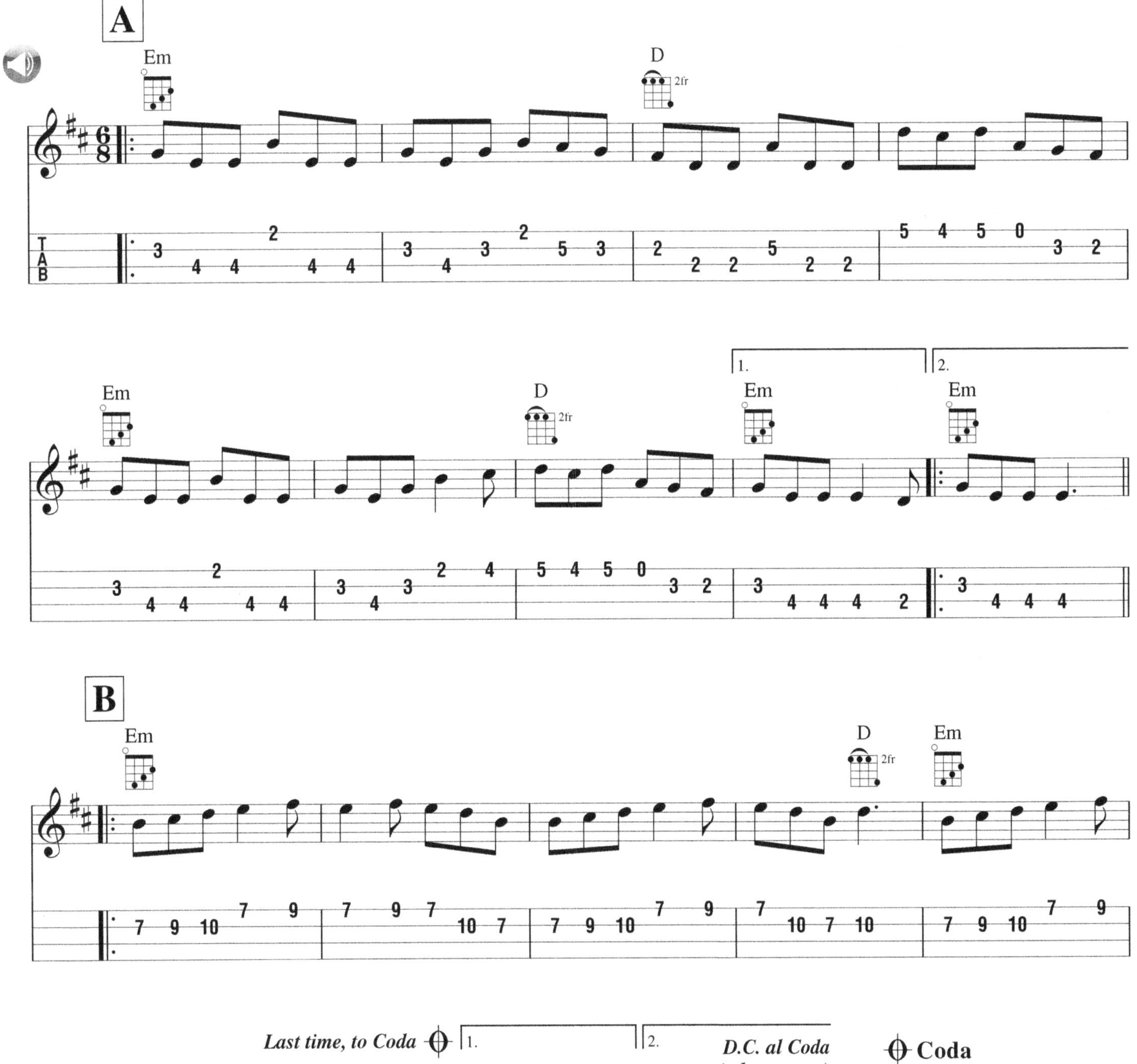

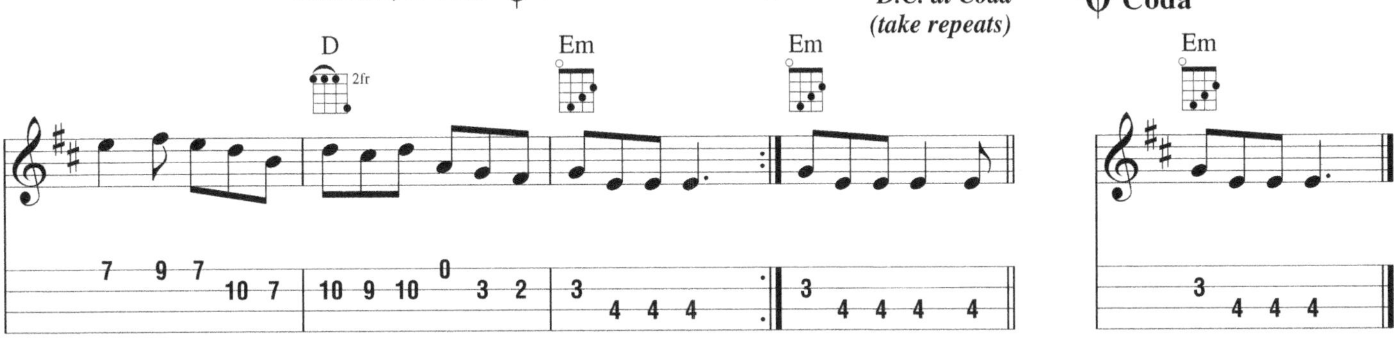

The Black Nag

This lovely English jig is performed as a single-line melody for section A, while section B consists of mostly descending arpeggios of a minor chord shape slid up and down the neck. It finishes up with a single-line phrase.

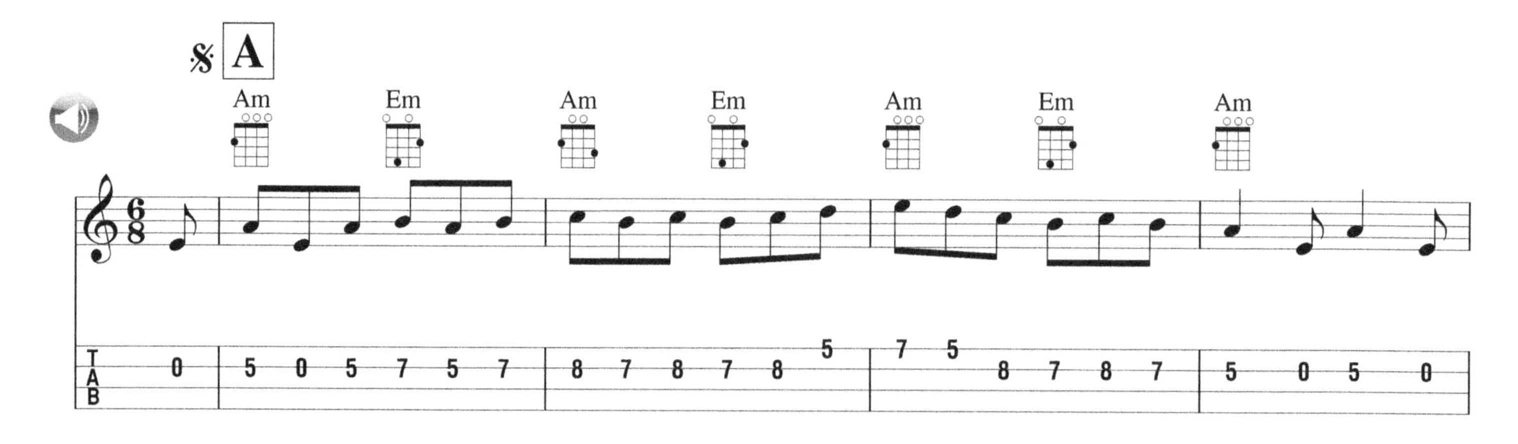

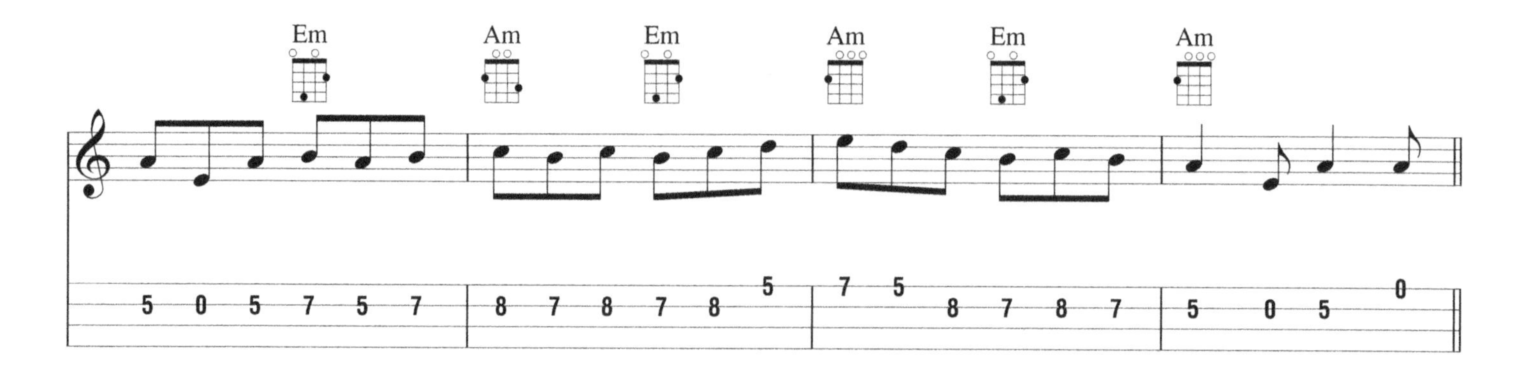

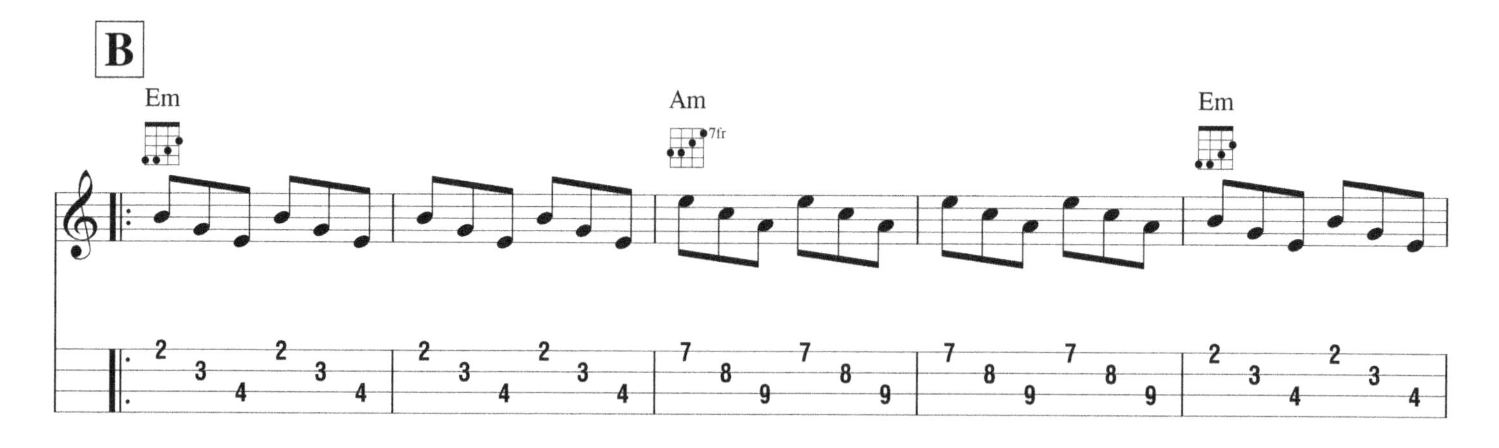

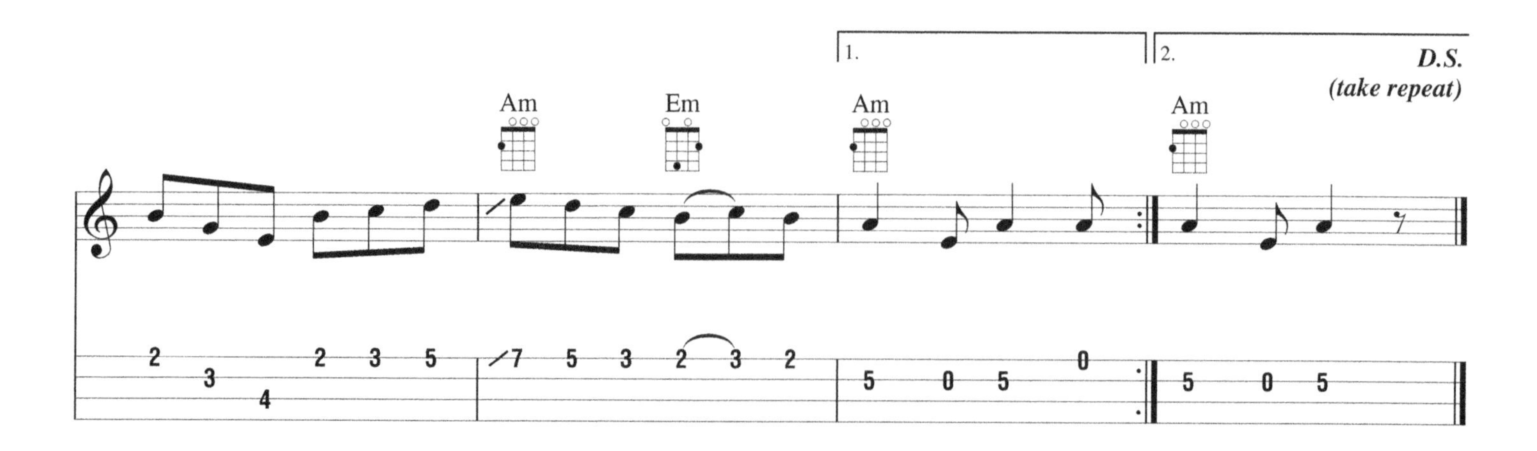

Morrison's Jig

An Irish session standard, this tune brings to mind fiddler James Morrison. He was a highly influential early recording artist and band leader. This arrangement is played fingerstyle. In the A section, the thumb plucks all the notes on the third string, with the middle finger covering the notes on the first string, and the index finger covering the second string. The B part is executed with a 7th-fret barre on the first three strings, held down throughout, and only released in the middle of measure 15 through measure 16, and the middle of measure 23 through measure 24.

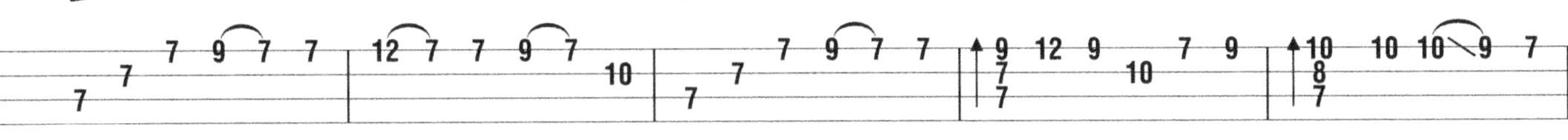

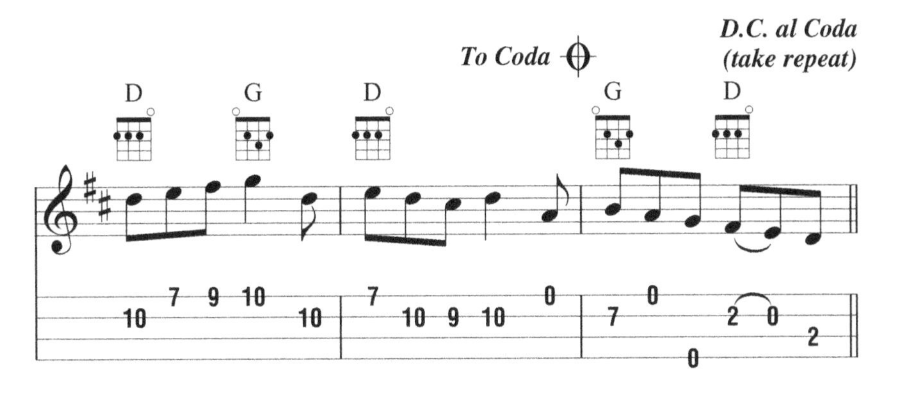

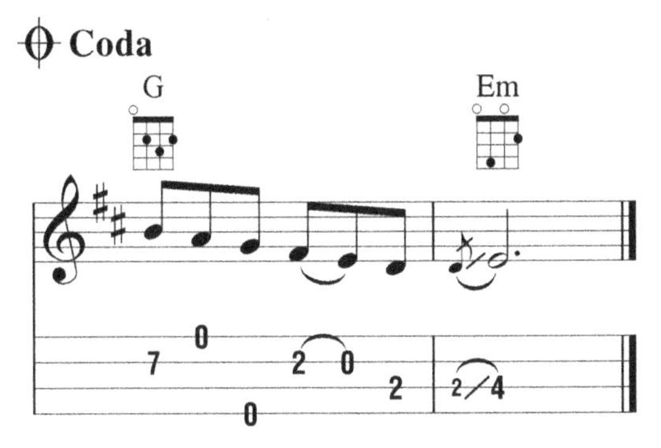

Gary Owen

This great Irish jig is arranged in the campanella style. It was rumored to be the favorite tune of General Armstrong Custer.

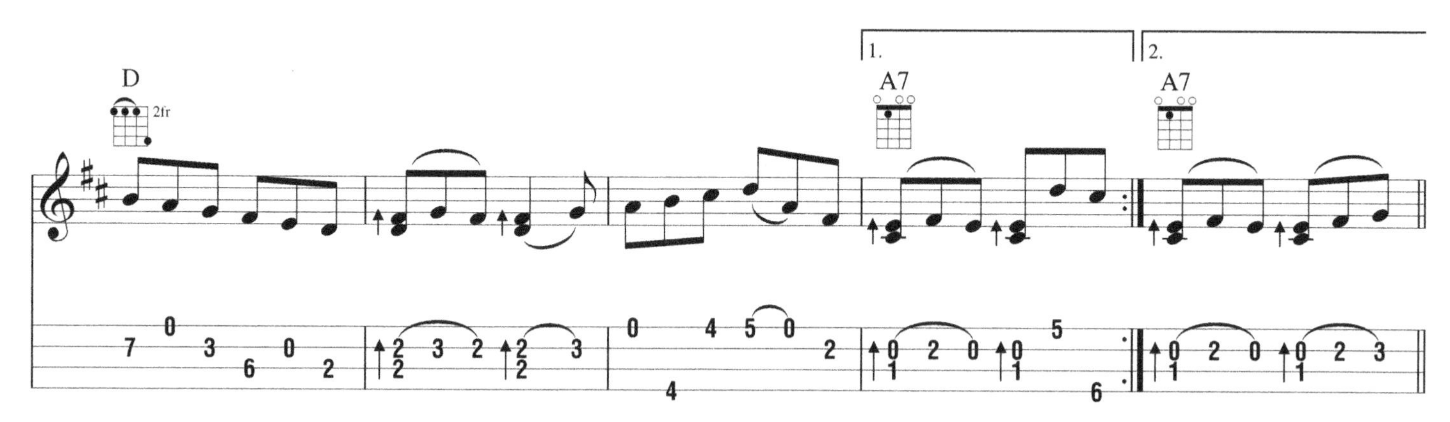

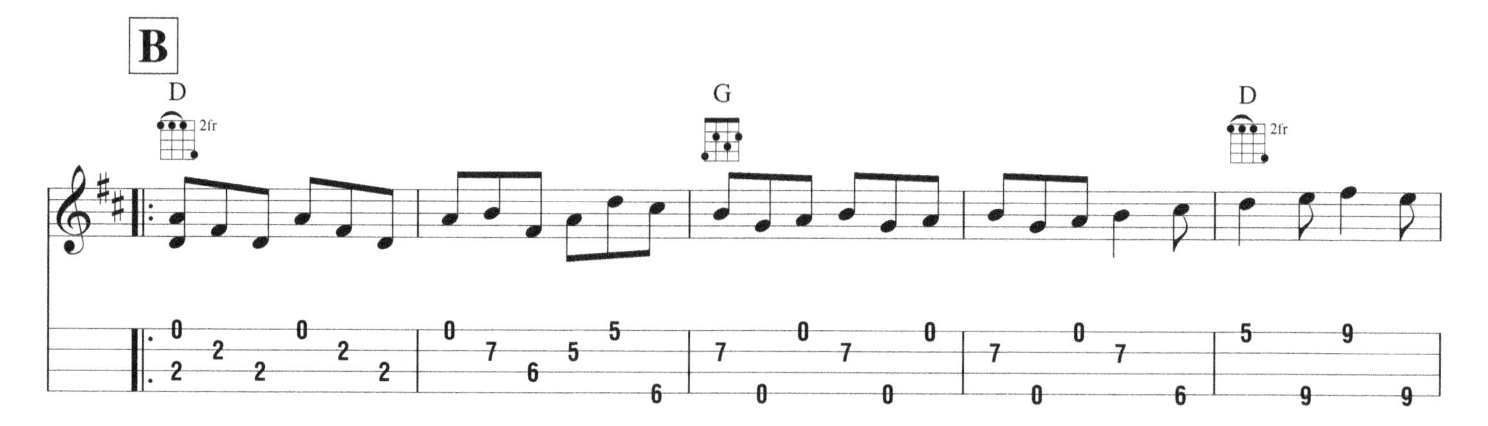

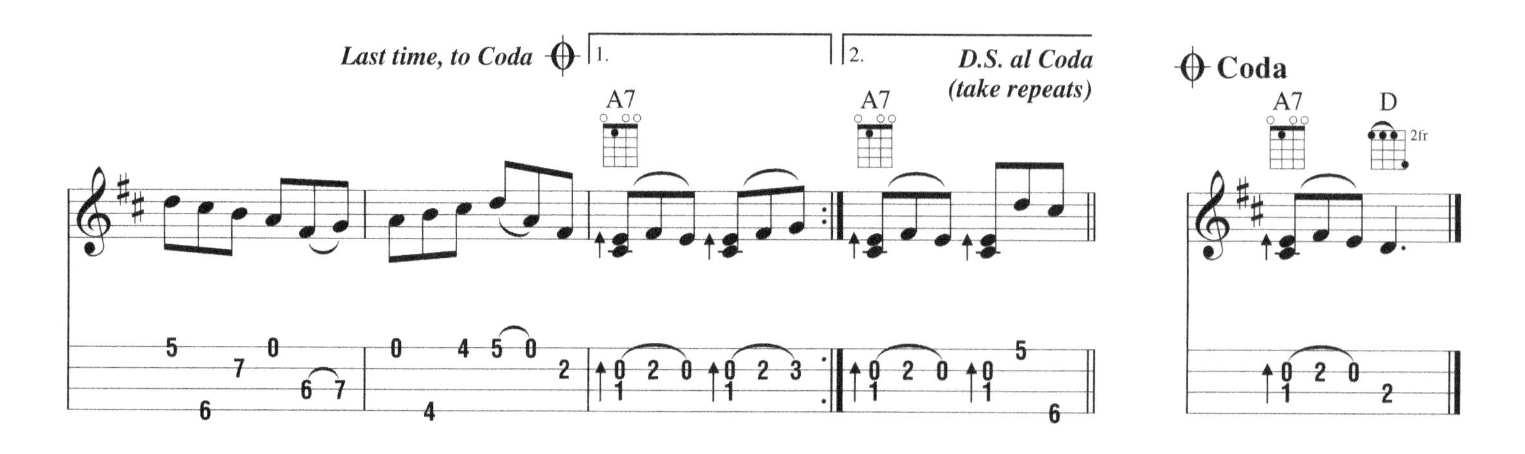

HORNPIPE

A *hornpipe* is a dance originating in the British Isles.

Harvest Home

This one is also called "The Cork Hornpipe." Hornpipes are usually performed at a moderate tempo, with a bit of a lilt or swing to them. This tune is played fingerstyle with a few arpeggiations and double-stops, however, it is mostly a single-note melody line. The open A string is often thrown in to accommodate some of the big melodic leaps between the fretted notes.

CHORDAL STYLE

Star of the County Down

"Star of the County Down" is an old Irish ballad. The first verse states, "In Bainbridge town near the County Down, one morning last July..." and goes on to talk about a young fella who chanced to meet a charming young lady, and forever thereafter, dreams of how one day they'll wed. It is simply a gorgeous melody and sounds dynamite on the ukulele as a chordal arrangement.

POLKA

A *polka* is a moderately quick Bohemian dance in 2/4 or cut time, characterized by a hop on the first beat.

Britches Full of Stitches

Here is a great Irish polka, played on the E and A strings as a single-line melody and incorporating a hefty dose of hammer-ons and pull-offs.

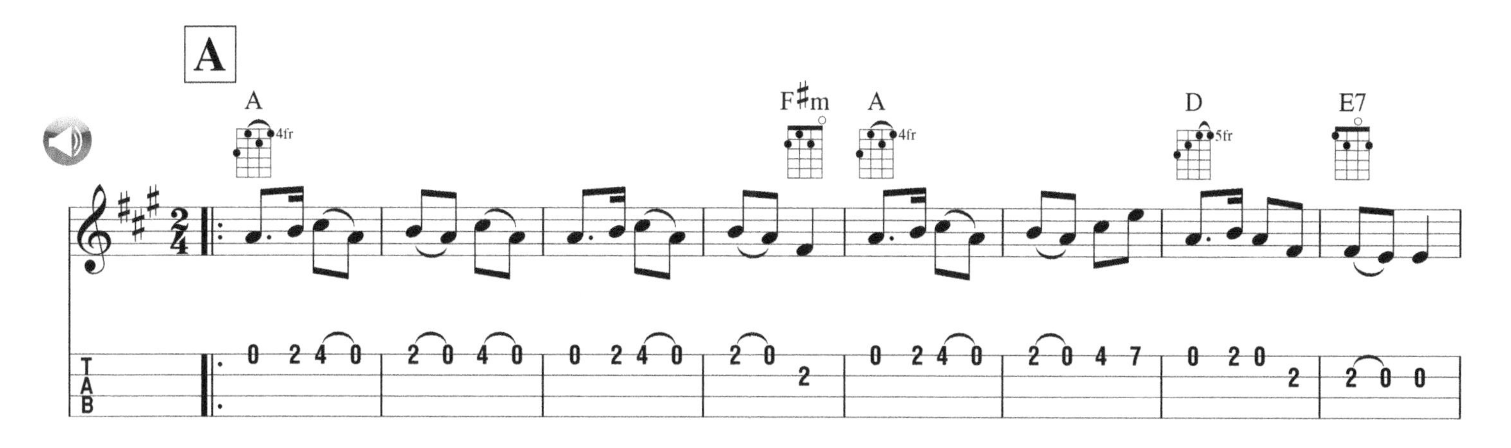

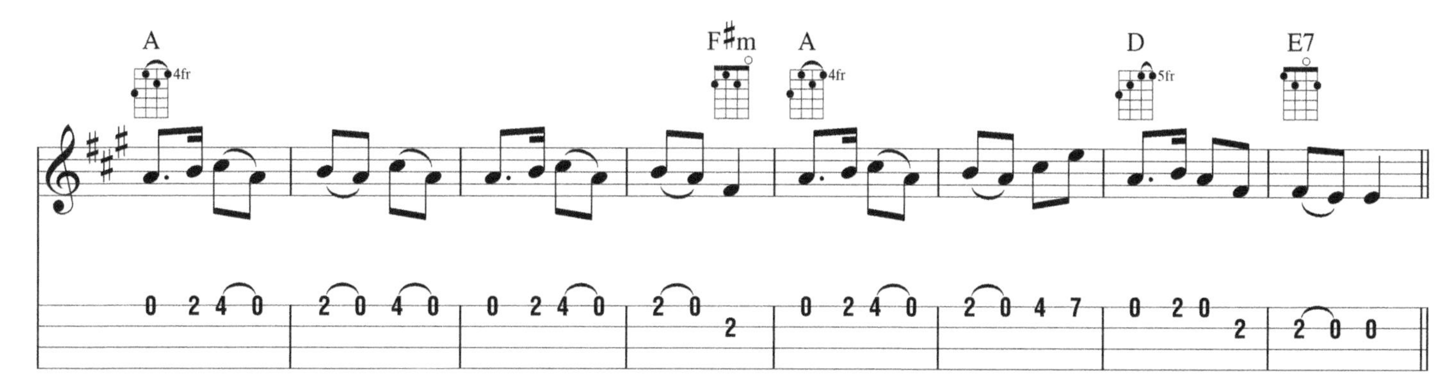

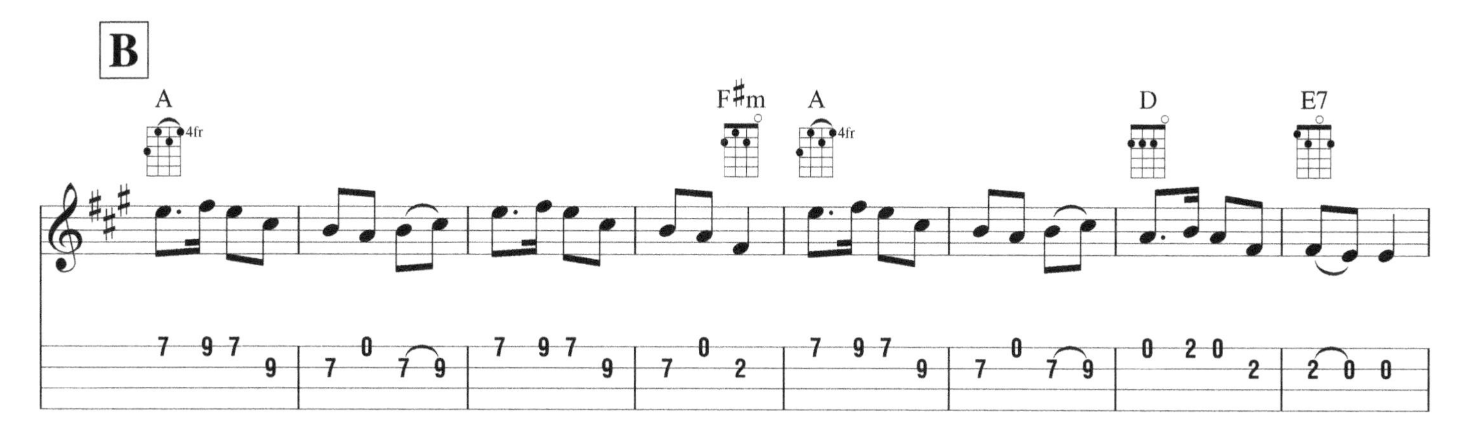

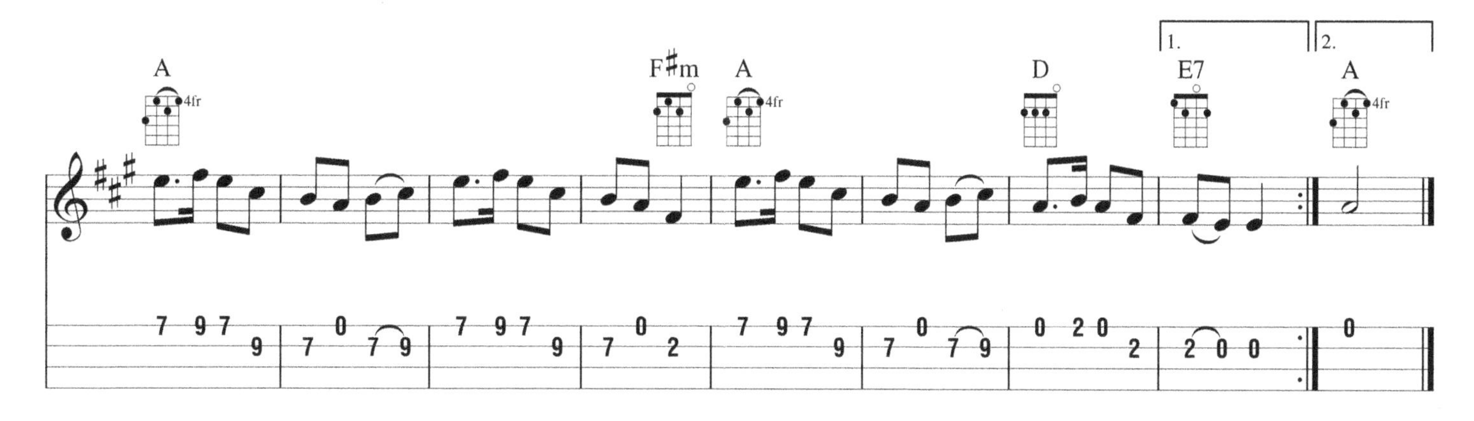

Kevin Burke is one of the great contemporary fiddlers of our time. Rooted in Irish traditions, his style encompasses musical influences from all over the world. (Photo courtesy of Kevin Burke, www.kevinburke.com)

Canada's virtuosic ambassador of the ukulele, James Hill. James is also a fiddle player who often performs reels, jigs, and hornpipes on his ukulele. (Photo courtesy of Kevin Kell)

CLAWHAMMER

Irish Polka

This tune is also called "Terry Tiehan's Polka." It is a standard Irish session piece. I have arranged it in the clawhammer style, so please review the Playing Tips page regarding this technique. Then, spend some time absorbing the melody on the audio track before you begin studying the tab and/or notation. Watch out for the pull-offs that appear throughout the tune, as well as the hammer-ons that appear in the B section only. Good luck and happy picking! – Lil' Rev

Old Molly Hare

Here is a clawhammer tune in G. This great old-time number seems to be related to the Irish tune, “The Fairy Reel.” It is often played in the key of D but I’ve heard versions in C, A, and F. Fiddler Paul Smith does a great, straight-ahead version in G. – John Nicholson

Old Molly Hare, what you doin’ thar?
Sitting on a hillside eatin’ on a pear.
Look back, look back, daddy caught a bear.
Comin’ down the hillside, Molly’s eatin’ pears.

Old Molly Hare, what you doin’ thar?
Diggin’ out a post hole, pulling out your hair.
Old Molly Hare, what you doin’ thar?
Runnin’ through the cotton patch far as I can tear.

The Elk Mountain String Band (Wikimedia Commons)

Dwight Lamb is a legendary Midwestern fiddle and button box player from Onowa, Iowa. He has some deep roots in the Missouri-style fiddle tradition à la Bob Walters. He also plays traditional Danish tunes on the single row button accordion which he learned as a kid from his grandfather Chris Jerup. (Photo courtesy of Mette Bebe)

Lil' Rev in San Francisco, CA, on his annual tour of the West Coast, circa 2011.

Hammond Breakdown

"The Hammond Breakdown" was composed in 1993 on a trip to New Orleans, Louisiana. John and I drove home in a '79 Bonneville and as we passed through the town of Hammond, LA this little ditty was born! It's played with the clawhammer technique. – Lil' Rev

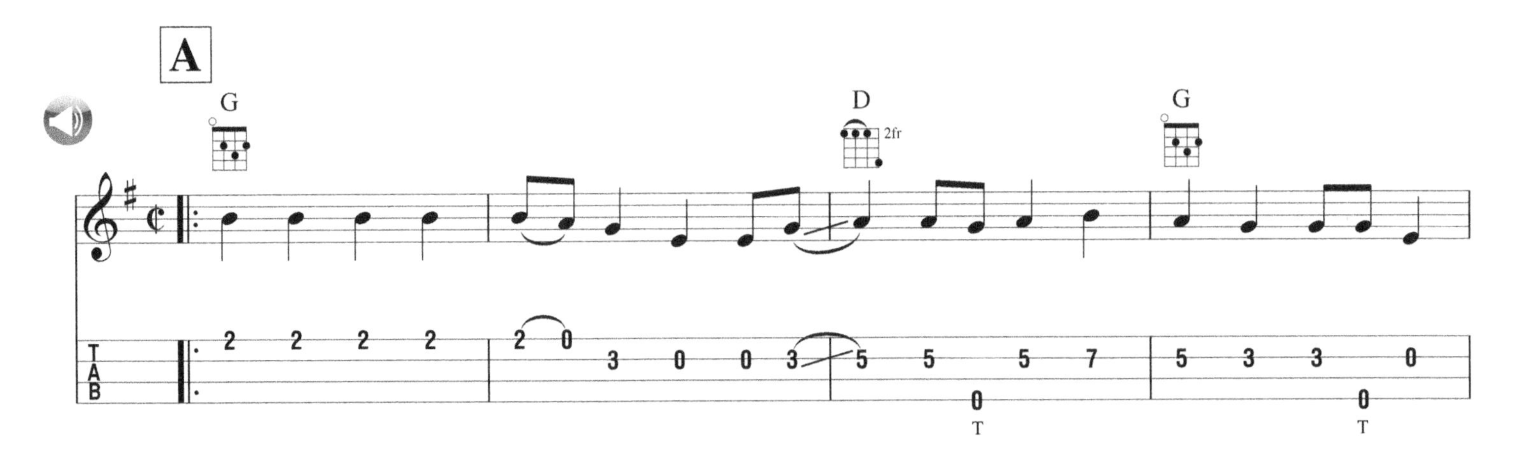

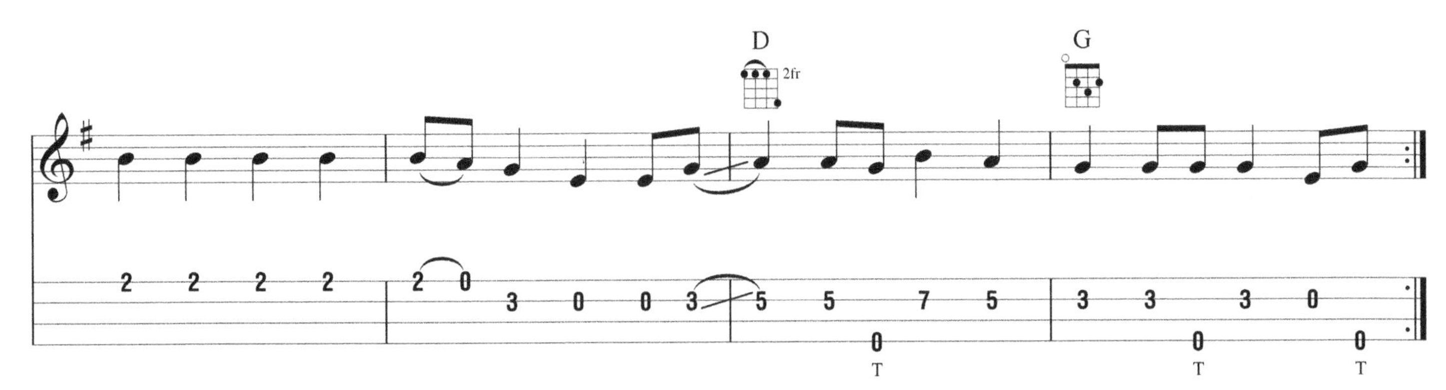

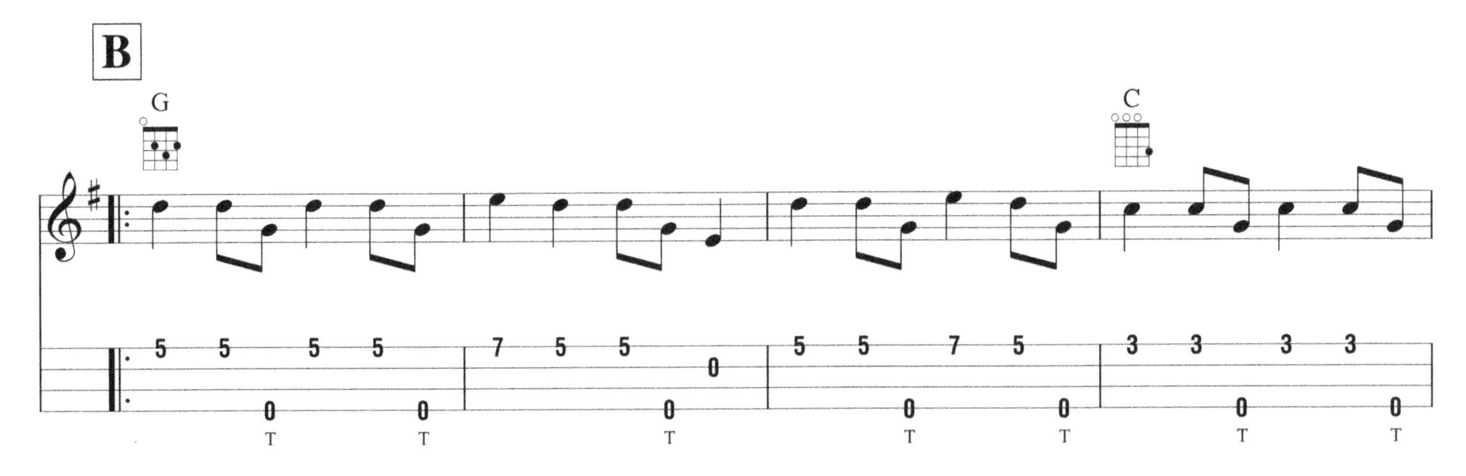

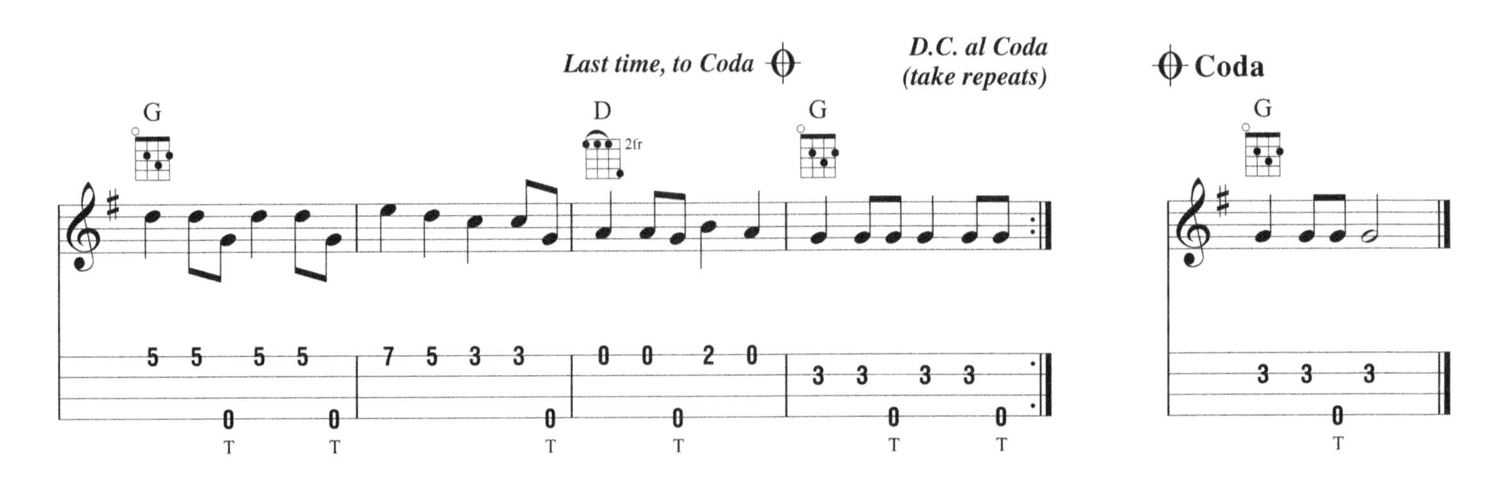

Sugar in the Coffee-O

Missouri fiddler Vesta Johnson plays a most charming version of this tune on the 1996 Rounder Records compilation, *Old-Time Music on the Air, Vol. 2.*

I learned this tune from fiddler and mandolinist Bruce "Gart" Gartner at the "Earful of Fiddle" fiddle camp in Mecosta, Michigan. – John Nicholson

Leather Britches

"Leather Breeches" was a nickname in some parts of the American South and West for green beans dried in the pod and later cooked.

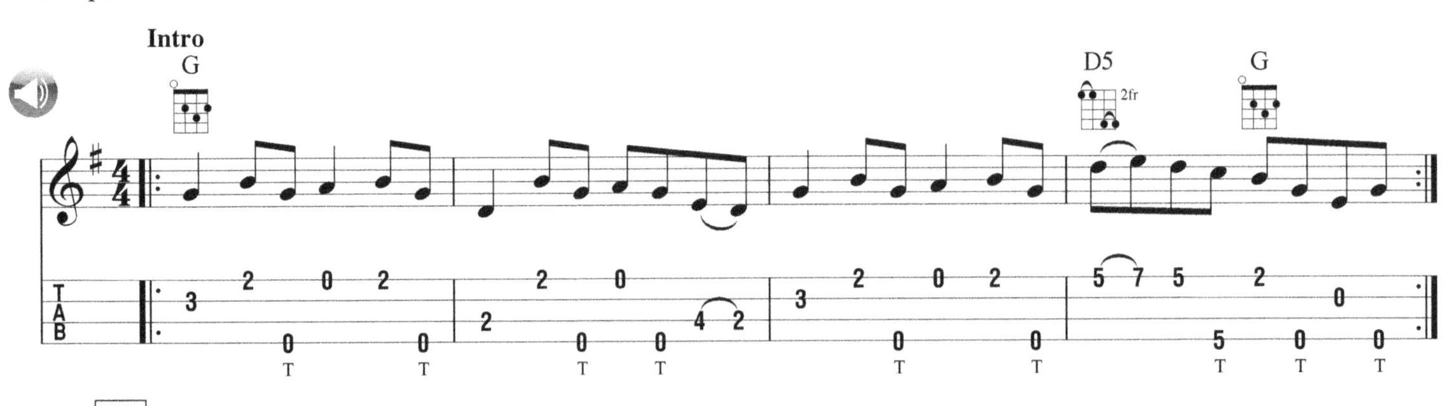

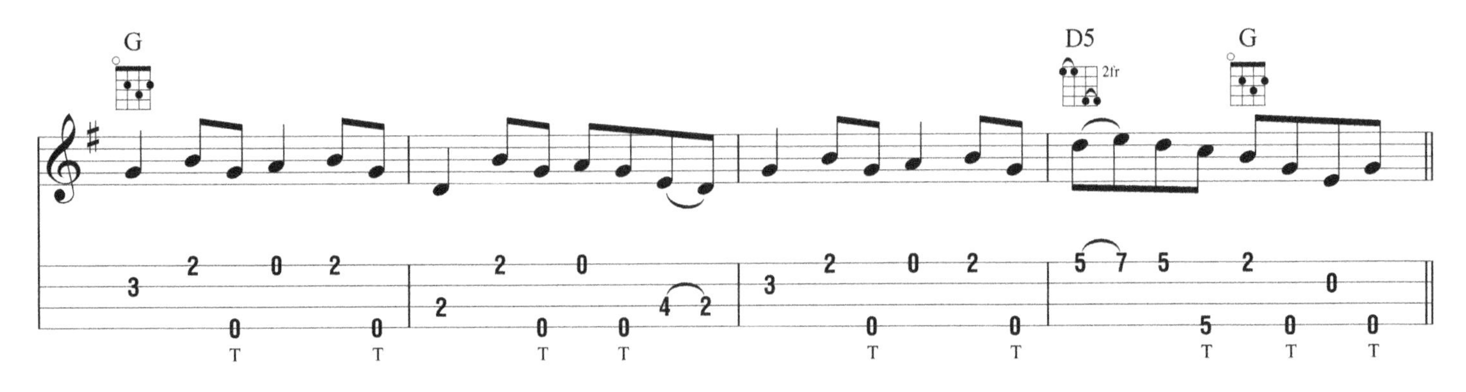

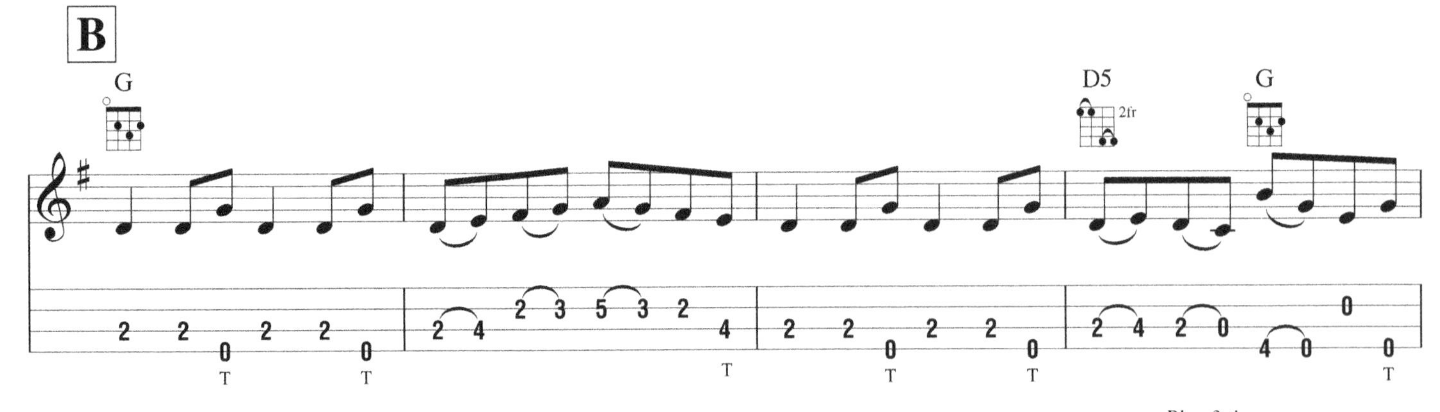

Lil' Rev with the late, great ukulele master John King

Lil' Rev (center) hanging out with the Canote Brothers, Greg and Jere, at the 2007 Portland Uke Festival.

Mountain Road

This lively Irish reel is arranged in a clawhammer style but could be picked in a single-string lead style just as effectively.

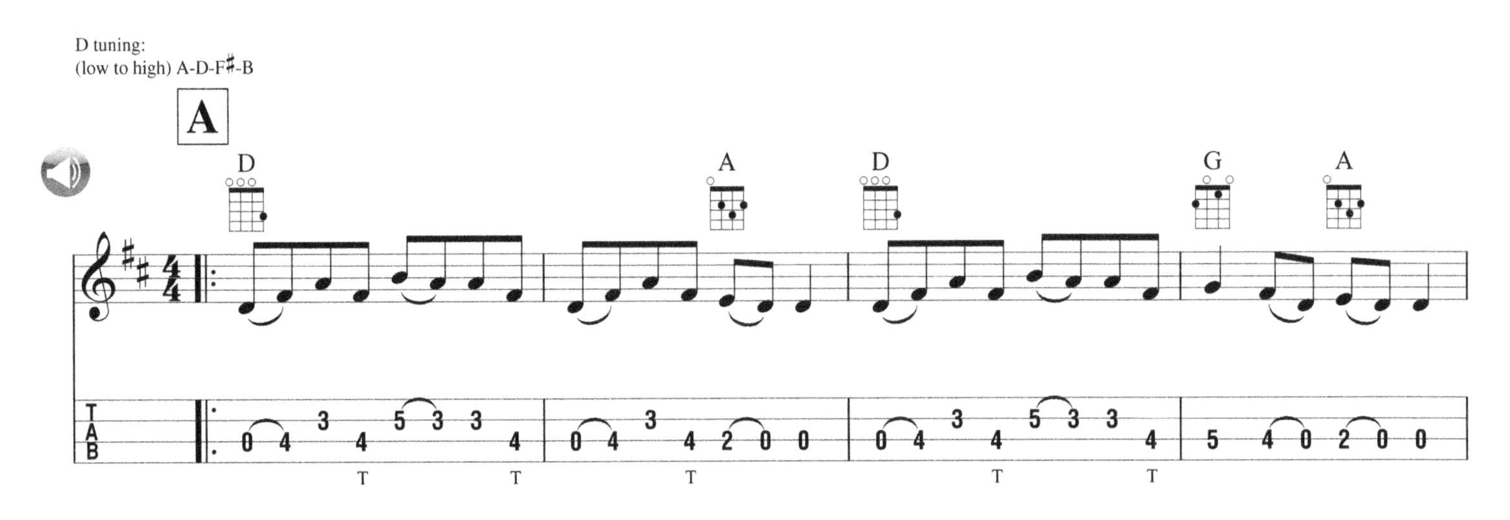

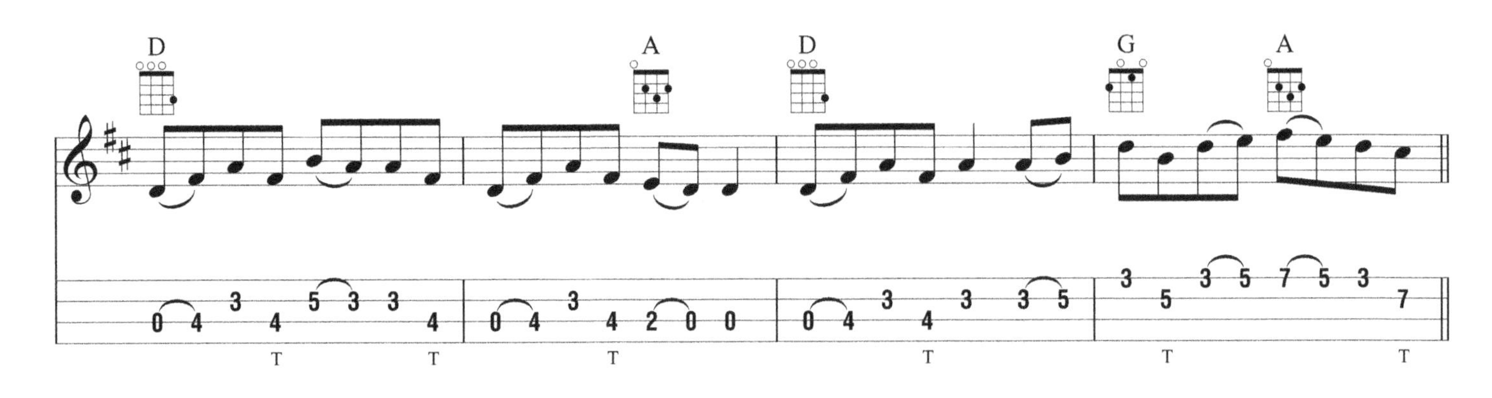

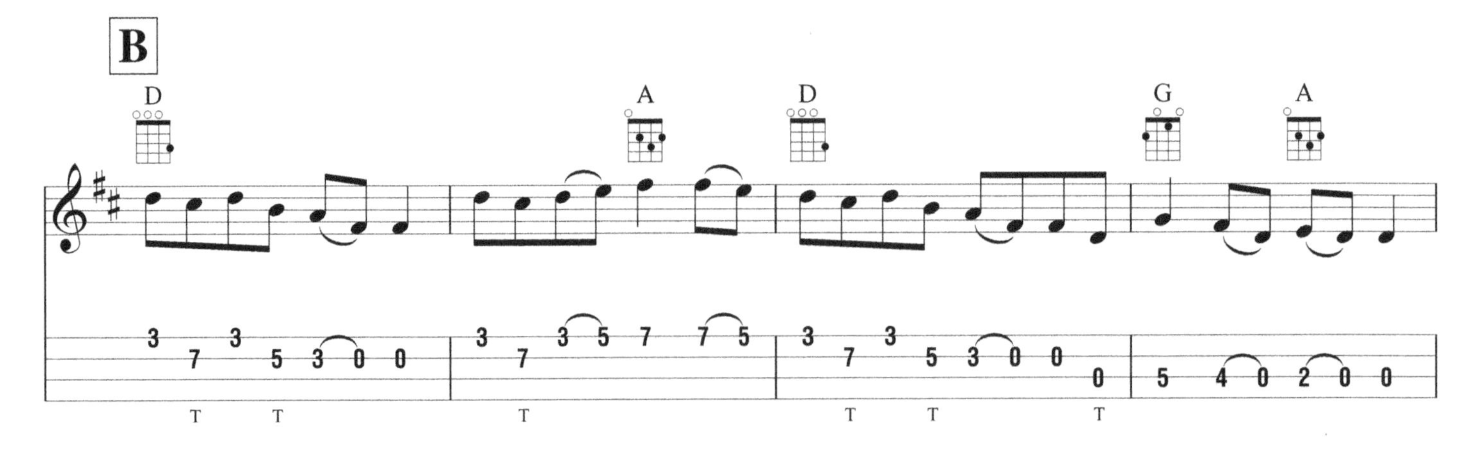

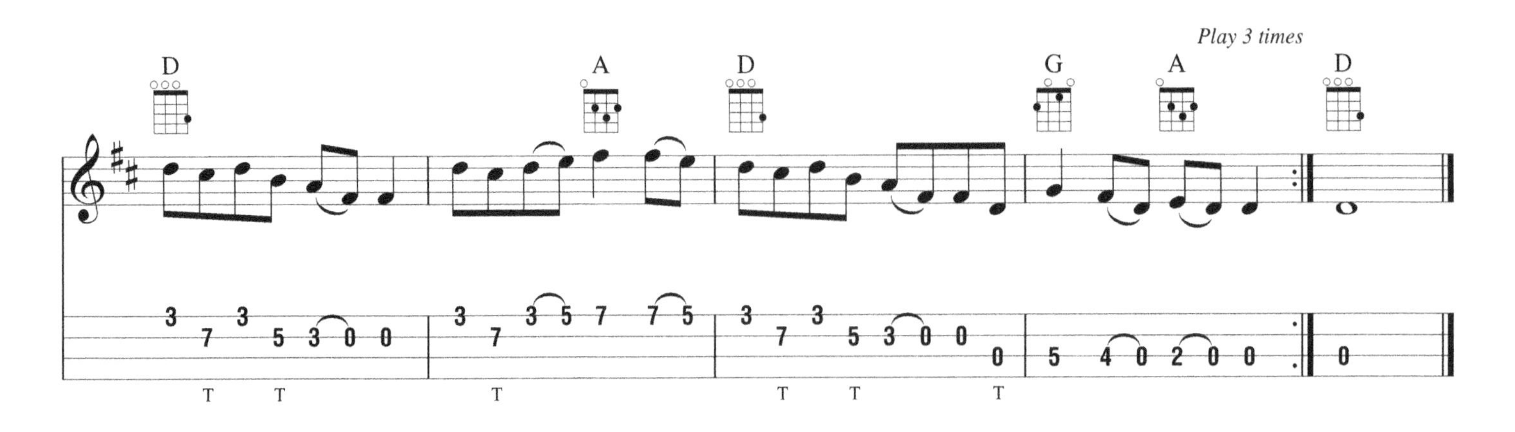

CONTEST PIECES

Fiddle contests have been held in America since colonial times. They often serve to assess who is the best fiddler of a given locale. Most often, players are required to perform a breakdown (reel), a waltz, and often a tune of choice—usually something flashy to demonstrate technical mastery.

Walworth County Breakdown

My mother's side of the family settled in Walworth County, Wisconsin in the 1840s. I wrote this tune while driving through Walworth County at sunset in early fall a few years back. The fields were aglow and large oaks lined the roads. It involves single-note picking with double-stops, pull-offs, and some chording.

– John Nicholson

Ragtime Annie

The last two tunes are very ornate with many parts. They are played fingerstyle, incorporating a host of techniques, including campanella, single-note style, double-stops, strumming, slides, hammer-ons, pull-offs, and arpeggios!

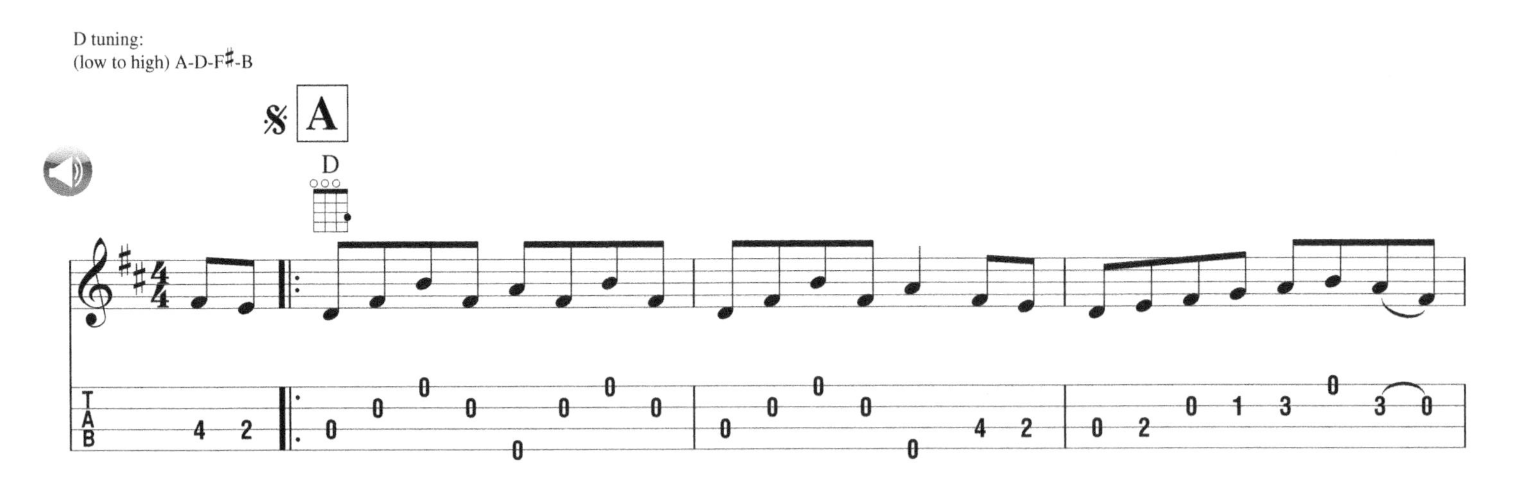

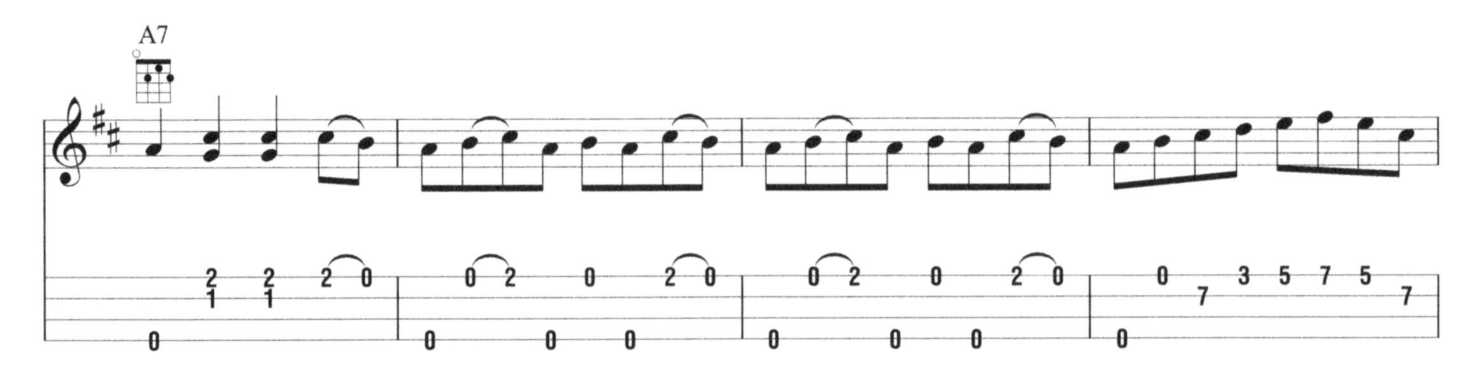

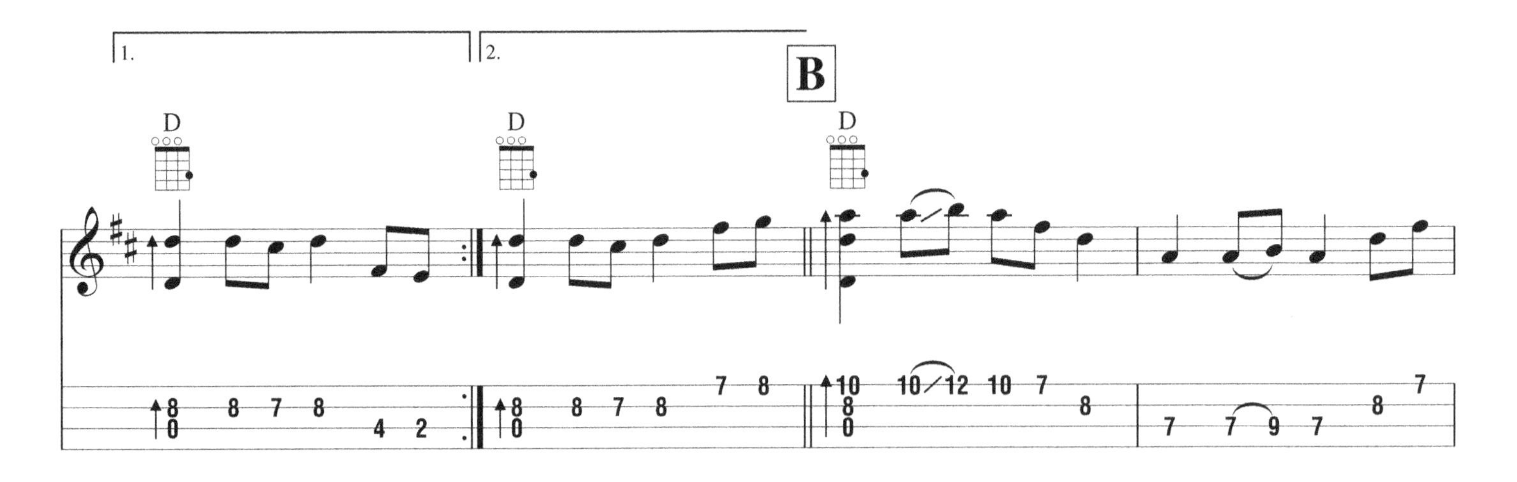

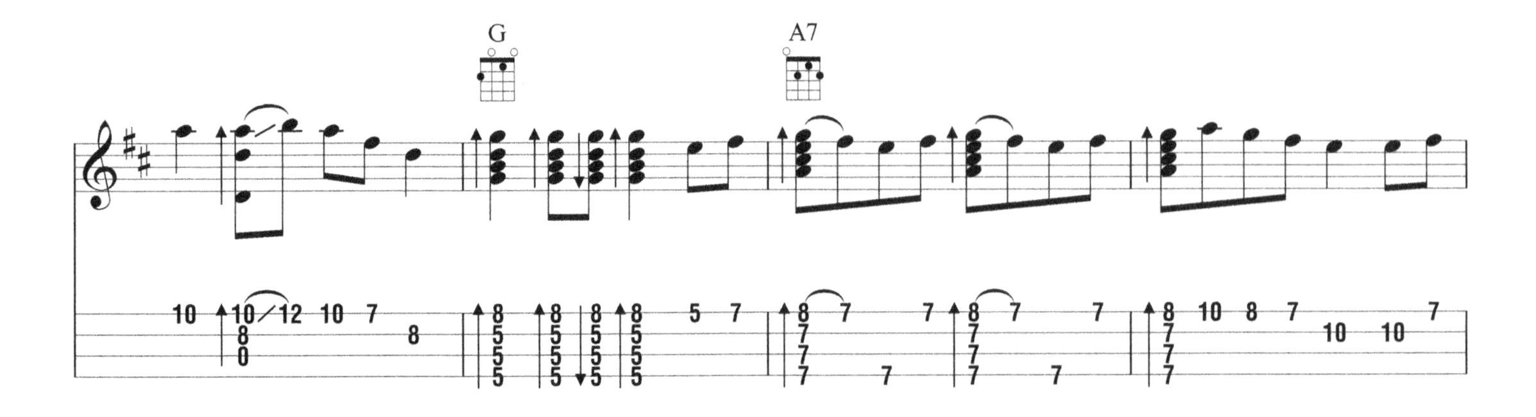

D

C
G
D

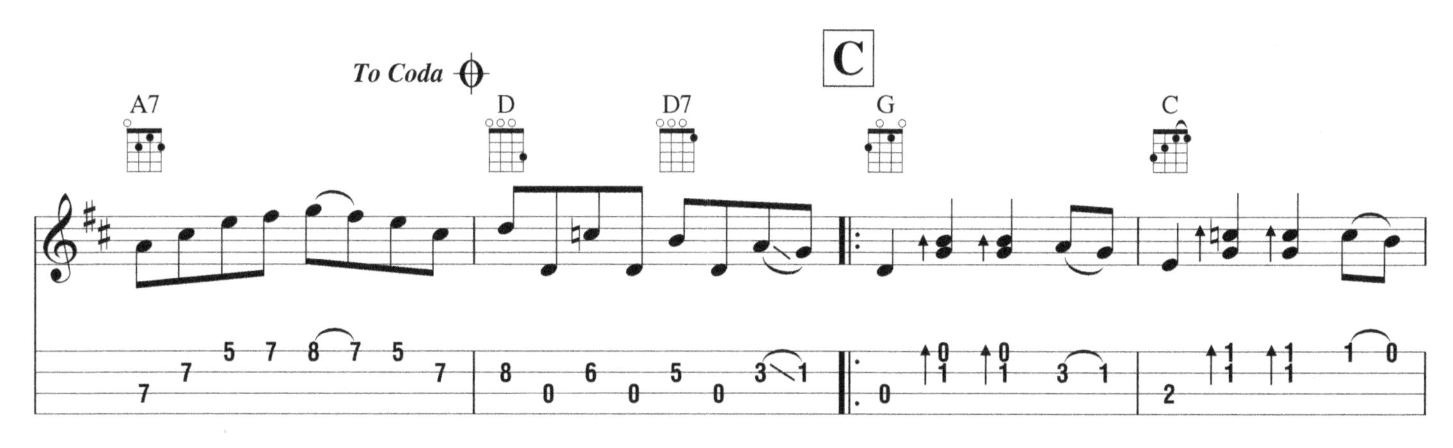
To Coda
C
A7
D
D7
G
C

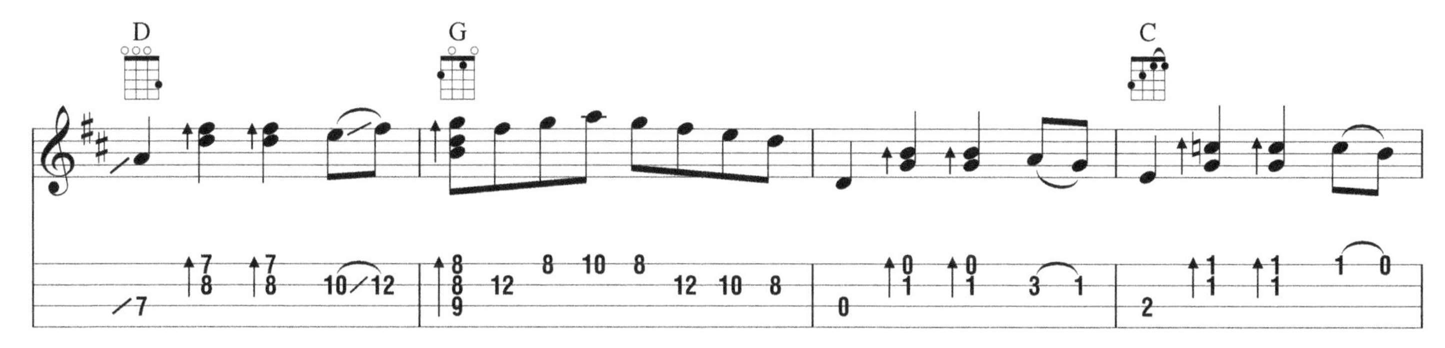
D
G
C

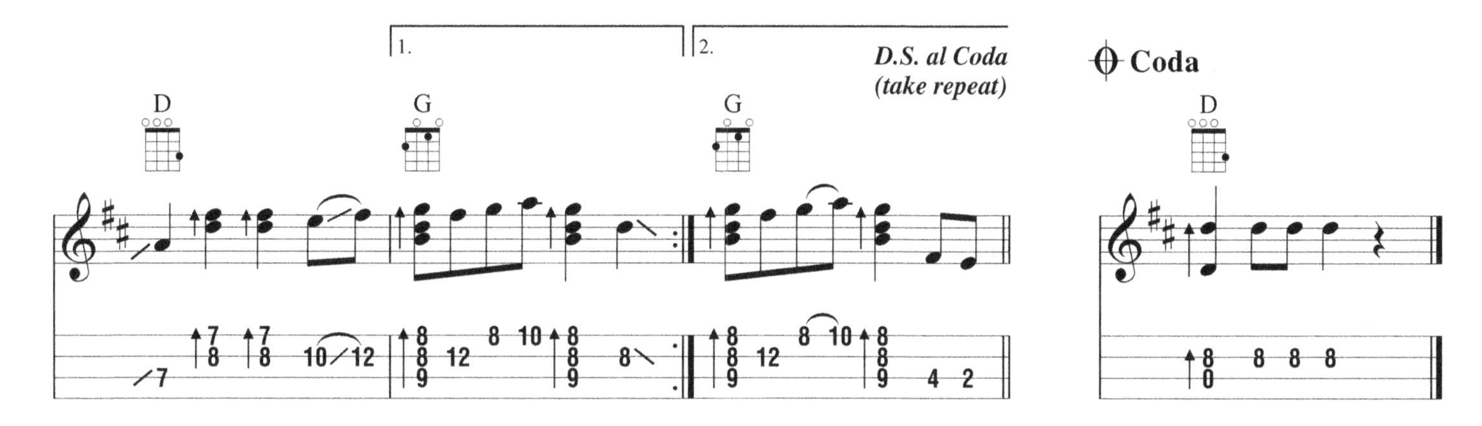
1.
2.
D.S. al Coda
(take repeat)
Coda
D
G
G
D

Say Old Man Can You Play a Ukulele?

"Say Old Man Can You Play a Ukulele?" starts out campanella style with the middle finger and thumb alternating between the first and fourth strings to pick the majority of the consecutive notes in the A section. The actual title of this tune is "Say Old Man Can You Play a Fiddle?" However, in this case…

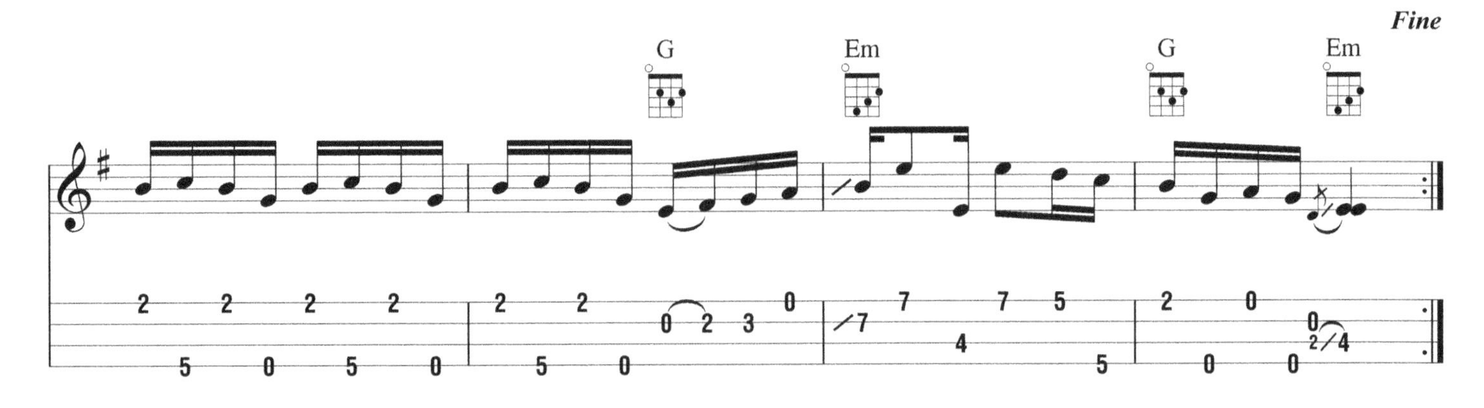

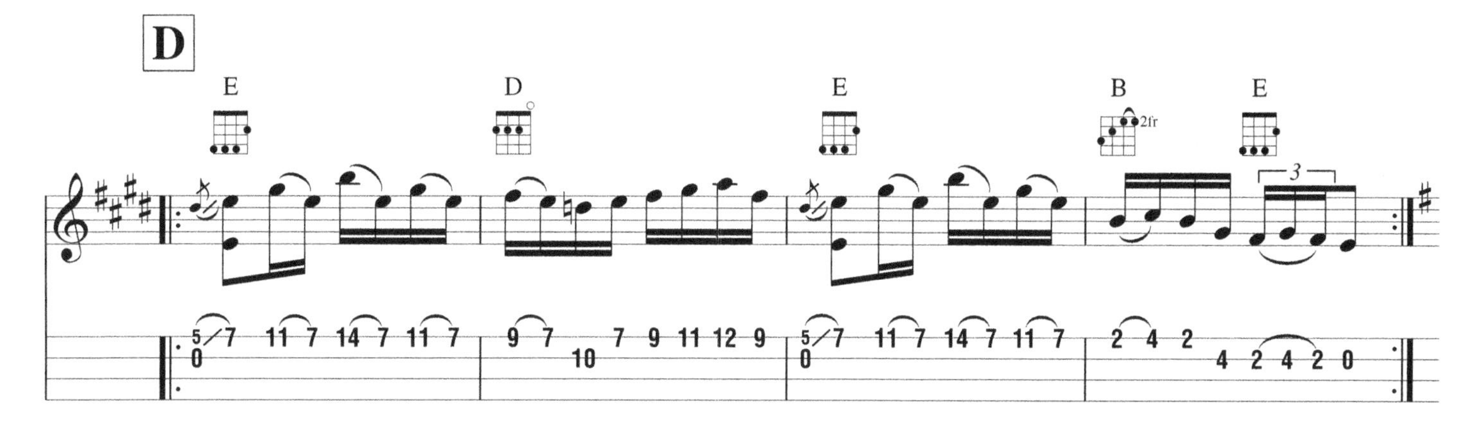
D
E
D
E
B
2fr
E
3

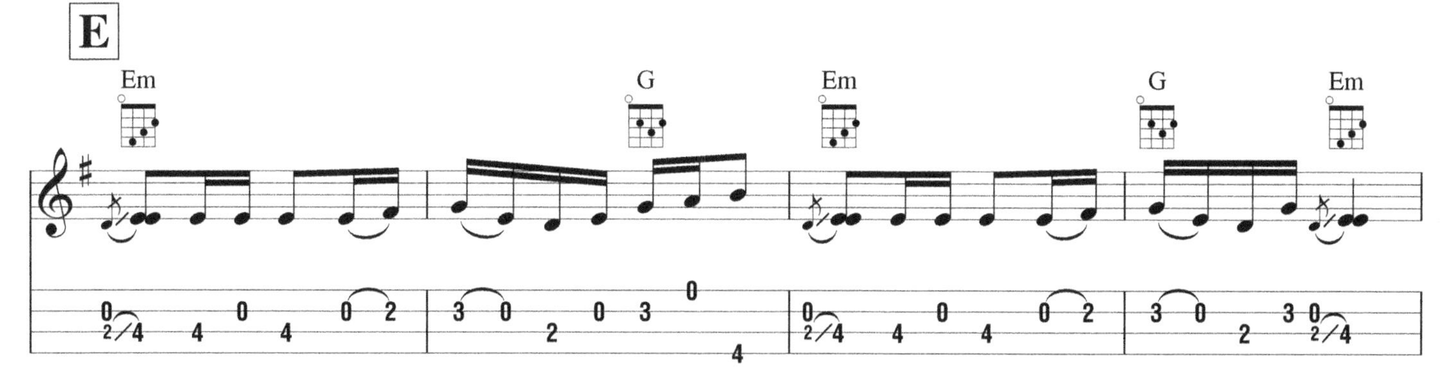
E
Em
G
Em
G
Em

G
Em
G
Em

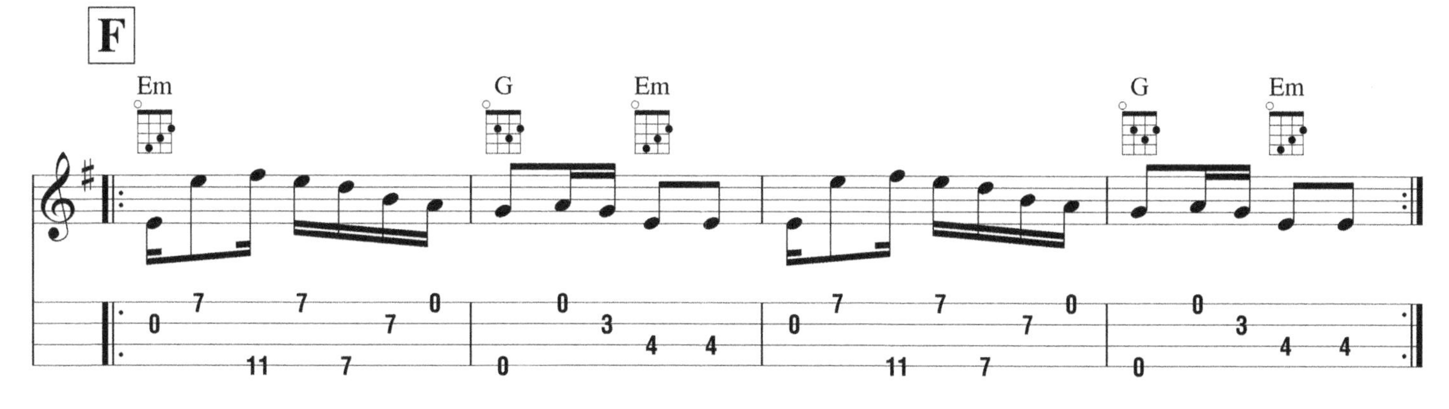
F
Em
G
Em
G
Em

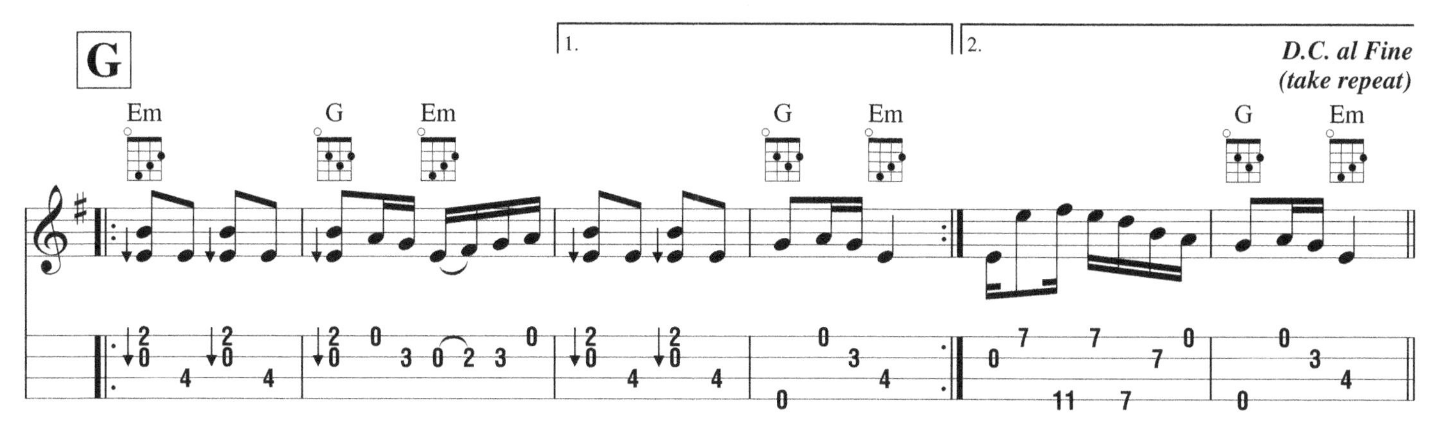
1.
2.
D.C. al Fine
(take repeat)
G
Em
G
Em
G
Em
G
Em

OLD TIME MUSIC RESOURCE GUIDE

Festivals:

Old Time Fiddlers Gathering at Battleground, IN: http://www.indianafiddlersgathering.org/
Old Fiddlers Convention at Galax, VA: http://www.oldfiddlersconvention.com/
Carter Fold: http://www.carterfamilyfold.org/
Centrum Fiddle & Dance Camp: http://centrum.org/festival-of-american-fiddle-tunes-artist-faculty/
Cliff Top (Appalachian String Band Music Festival): http://www.wvculture.org/stringband/
National Old Time Fiddlers Contest at Weiser, ID: http://www.fiddlecontest.org/
Milwaukee Irish Festival: http://irishfest.com/Irishfest.htm
Earful of Fiddle: http://www.earfuloffiddle.com

Fiddle & Dance Organizations:

Chicago Barn Dance: http://www.chicagobarndance.org/
New England Contra Dance Links: http://www.contradancelinks.com/newengland.html
Missouri State Old Time Fiddlers Association: http://www.missourifiddling.com/
Wheatland Music Organization (MI Dance): http://www.wheatlandmusic.org/
Portland Contra Dance: http://www.portlandcountrydance.org/Dances.htm
Seattle Contra: http://seattledance.org/contra
Texas Old Time Fiddlers: http://www.totfa.org/
Texas Squares: http://www.squaredancetx.com/
Wisconsin Polka: http://www.wisconsinpolkamusic.com/
Minnesota Fiddlers Association: http://www.fiddlemn.com/
Ashokan Music & Dance Camps: http://ashokan.org/camps/

Fiddlin' Powers and Family
(photo courtesy of Southern Folklife Collection, Wilson Library,
The University of North Carolina at Chapel Hill)

ABOUT THE AUTHORS

Lil' Rev & John Nicholson met in Milwaukee, WI in the early 1990s. Their shared love of old-time blues, folk, and traditional music styles helped forge a dynamic duo which carried them far and wide to festivals, pubs, street corners, theaters, and restaurants all over the Midwest. In 1996, they were voted "Best Acoustic Act in Milwaukee" by *The Shepherd Express* reader's choice awards and soon thereafter helped found the award-winning string band, Frogwater.

John Nicholson is widely regarded as a walking encyclopedia of American roots guitar styles from Delta blues to Celtic, classical, roots rock, and more! He is a multi-instrumentalist who performs on banjo, mandolin, tiple, ukulele, and guitar. John has taught guitar at the University of Wisconsin-Milwaukee Continuing Education Program for over 13 years as well as Milwaukee's Irish Fest Summer School, Wheatland Traditional Arts Weekend, and privately. An ardent participant in Milwaukee's world class theater community, John has written and performed with Renaissance Theaterworks and First Stage Children's Theater. He is the author of another Hal Leonard book, *Play Ukulele Today! Level 2*, and arranger for *J.S. Bach for Fingerstyle Ukulele*. John is a vibrant part of Wisconsin's traditional music scene, performing regularly with his wife Susan in Frogwater. You can reach him at: www.frogwater.us/index.asp or blindspot130@yahoo.com.

Lil' Rev is often hailed as one of the hardest-working ukulele instructors on the mainland, logging over 35,000 miles annually. He is the author of the *Hal Leonard Ukulele Method* series, *101 Ukulele Licks*, *Easy Songs for Ukulele*, *Hal Leonard Baritone Ukulele Method* and *Play Harmonica Today!* An award-winning multi-instrumentalist, poet, and storyteller, he performs his historical one-man musical shows on quilting, Yiddish, and Tin Pan Alley at theaters, festivals, and museums all over the continental U.S. He can be reached at: www.lilrev.com or fountainofuke.blogspot.com.

The authors wish to thank the following individuals, without all of whom this project would never have come to be: Susan Nicholson, Will Branch, Jennifer Rupp, Scott Finch, and all of the good folks at Hal Leonard.

UKULELE CHORD SONGBOOKS

This series features convenient 6" x 9" books with complete lyrics and chord symbols for dozens of great songs. Each song also includes chord grids at the top of every page and the first notes of the melody for easy reference.

ACOUSTIC ROCK

60 tunes: American Pie • Band on the Run • Catch the Wind • Daydream • Every Rose Has Its Thorn • Hallelujah • Iris • More Than Words • Patience • The Sound of Silence • Space Oddity • Sweet Talkin' Woman • Wake up Little Susie • Who'll Stop the Rain • and more.
00702482 ....$15.99

THE BEATLES

100 favorites: Across the Universe • Carry That Weight • Dear Prudence • Good Day Sunshine • Here Comes the Sun • If I Fell • Love Me Do • Michelle • Ob-La-Di, Ob-La-Da • Revolution • Something • Ticket to Ride • We Can Work It Out • and many more.
00703065..$19.99

BEST SONGS EVER

70 songs: All I Ask of You • Bewitched • Edelweiss • Just the Way You Are • Let It Be • Memory • Moon River • Over the Rainbow • Someone to Watch over Me • Unchained Melody • You Are the Sunshine of My Life • You Raise Me Up • and more.
00117050 ....$16.99

CHILDREN'S SONGS

80 classics: Alphabet Song • "C" Is for Cookie • Do-Re-Mi • I'm Popeye the Sailor Man • Mickey Mouse March • Oh! Susanna • Polly Wolly Doodle • Puff the Magic Dragon • The Rainbow Connection • Sing • Three Little Fishies (Itty Bitty Poo) • and many more.
00702473 ....$14.99

CHRISTMAS CAROLS

75 favorites: Away in a Manger • Coventry Carol • The First Noel • Good King Wenceslas • Hark! the Herald Angels Sing • I Saw Three Ships • Joy to the World • O Little Town of Bethlehem • Still, Still, Still • Up on the Housetop • What Child Is This? • and more.
00702474 ....$14.99

CHRISTMAS SONGS

55 Christmas classics: Do They Know It's Christmas? • Frosty the Snow Man • Happy Xmas (War Is Over) • Jingle-Bell Rock • Little Saint Nick • The Most Wonderful Time of the Year • White Christmas • and more.
00101776 ....$14.99

ISLAND SONGS

60 beach party tunes: Blue Hawaii • Day-O (The Banana Boat Song) • Don't Worry, Be Happy • Island Girl • Kokomo • Lovely Hula Girl • Mele Kalikimaka • Red, Red Wine • Surfer Girl • Tiny Bubbles • Ukulele Lady • and many more.
00702471 ....$16.99

150 OF THE MOST BEAUTIFUL SONGS EVER

150 melodies: Always • Bewitched • Candle in the Wind • Endless Love • In the Still of the Night • Just the Way You Are • Memory • The Nearness of You • People • The Rainbow Connection • Smile • Unchained Melody • What a Wonderful World • Yesterday • and more.
00117051 ....$24.99

PETER, PAUL & MARY

Over 40 songs: And When I Die • Blowin' in the Wind • Goodnight, Irene • If I Had a Hammer (The Hammer Song) • Leaving on a Jet Plane • Puff the Magic Dragon • This Land Is Your Land • We Shall Overcome • Where Have All the Flowers Gone? • and more.
00121822 ....$14.99

THREE CHORD SONGS

60 songs: Bad Case of Loving You • Bang a Gong (Get It On) • Blue Suede Shoes • Cecilia • Get Back • Hound Dog • Kiss • Me and Bobby McGee • Not Fade Away • Rock This Town • Sweet Home Chicago • Twist and Shout • You Are My Sunshine • and more.
00702483 ....$15.99

TOP HITS

31 hits: The A Team • Born This Way • Forget You • Ho Hey • Jar of Hearts • Little Talks • Need You Now • Rolling in the Deep • Teenage Dream • Titanium • We Are Never Ever Getting Back Together • and more.
00115929 ....$14.99

Prices, contents, and availability subject to change without notice.

www.halleonard.com

0222
238

HAL•LEONARD® UKULELE PLAY-ALONG

Now you can play your favorite songs on your uke with great-sounding backing tracks to help you sound like a bona fide pro! The audio also features playback tools so you can adjust the tempo without changing the pitch and loop challenging parts.

1. POP HITS
00701451 Book/CD Pack $15.99

3. HAWAIIAN FAVORITES
00701453 Book/Online Audio $14.99

4. CHILDREN'S SONGS
00701454 Book/Online Audio $14.99

5. CHRISTMAS SONGS
00701696 Book/CD Pack $12.99

6. LENNON & MCCARTNEY
00701723 Book/Online Audio $12.99

7. DISNEY FAVORITES
00701724 Book/Online Audio $14.99

8. CHART HITS
00701745 Book/CD Pack $15.99

9. THE SOUND OF MUSIC
00701784 Book/CD Pack $14.99

10. MOTOWN
00701964 Book/CD Pack $12.99

11. CHRISTMAS STRUMMING
00702458 Book/Online Audio $12.99

12. BLUEGRASS FAVORITES
00702584 Book/CD Pack $12.99

13. UKULELE SONGS
00702599 Book/CD Pack $12.99

14. JOHNNY CASH
00702615 Book/Online Audio $15.99

15. COUNTRY CLASSICS
00702834 Book/CD Pack $12.99

16. STANDARDS
00702835 Book/CD Pack $12.99

17. POP STANDARDS
00702836 Book/CD Pack $12.99

18. IRISH SONGS
00703086 Book/Online Audio $12.99

19. BLUES STANDARDS
00703087 Book/CD Pack $12.99

20. FOLK POP ROCK
00703088 Book/CD Pack $12.99

21. HAWAIIAN CLASSICS
00703097 Book/CD Pack $12.99

22. ISLAND SONGS
00703098 Book/CD Pack $12.99

23. TAYLOR SWIFT
00221966 Book/Online Audio $16.99

24. WINTER WONDERLAND
00101871 Book/CD Pack $12.99

25. GREEN DAY
00110398 Book/CD Pack $14.99

26. BOB MARLEY
00110399 Book/Online Audio $14.99

27. TIN PAN ALLEY
00116358 Book/CD Pack $12.99

28. STEVIE WONDER
00116736 Book/CD Pack $14.99

29. OVER THE RAINBOW & OTHER FAVORITES
00117076 Book/Online Audio $15.99

30. ACOUSTIC SONGS
00122336 Book/CD Pack $14.99

31. JASON MRAZ
00124166 Book/CD Pack $14.99

32. TOP DOWNLOADS
00127507 Book/CD Pack $14.99

33. CLASSICAL THEMES
00127892 Book/Online Audio $14.99

34. CHRISTMAS HITS
00128602 Book/CD Pack $14.99

35. SONGS FOR BEGINNERS
00129009 Book/Online Audio $14.99

36. ELVIS PRESLEY HAWAII
00138199 Book/Online Audio $14.99

37. LATIN
00141191 Book/Online Audio $14.99

38. JAZZ
00141192 Book/Online Audio $14.99

39. GYPSY JAZZ
00146559 Book/Online Audio $15.99

40. TODAY'S HITS
00160845 Book/Online Audio $14.99

HAL•LEONARD®
www.halleonard.com

Prices, contents, and availability subject to change without notice.

1021
483

The Best Songs Ever

70 songs have now been arranged for ukulele. Includes: Always • Bohemian Rhapsody • Memory • My Favorite Things • Over the Rainbow • Piano Man • What a Wonderful World • Yesterday • You Raise Me Up • and more.

00282413........$17.99

Campfire Songs for Ukulele

30 favorites to sing as you roast marshmallows and strum your uke around the campfire. Includes: God Bless the U.S.A. • Hallelujah • The House of the Rising Sun • I Walk the Line • Puff the Magic Dragon • Wagon Wheel • You Are My Sunshine • and more.

00129170 ....$14.99

The Daily Ukulele

arr. Liz and Jim Beloff

Strum a different song everyday with easy arrangements of 365 of your favorite songs in one big songbook! Includes favorites by the Beatles, Beach Boys, and Bob Dylan, folk songs, pop songs, kids' songs, Christmas carols, and Broadway and Hollywood tunes, all with a spiral binding for ease of use.

00240356 Original Edition.................$39.99
00240681 Leap Year Edition $39.99
00119270 Portable Edition $37.50

Disney Hits for Ukulele

Play 23 of your favorite Disney songs on your ukulele. Includes: The Bare Necessities • Cruella De Vil • Do You Want to Build a Snowman? • Kiss the Girl • Lava • Let It Go • Once upon a Dream • A Whole New World • and more.

00151250 ....$16.99

Also av[illegible]
[illegible] [illegible]ey Fun Songs for Ukulele ...$16.9[illegible]
[illegible] [illegible]sney Songs for Ukulele.......$14.99
[illegible] [illegible]irst 50 Disney Songs on Ukulele .$16.99

First 50 Songs You Should Play on Ukulele

An amazing collec-tion of 50 accessible, must-know favorites: Edelweiss • Hey, Soul Sister • I Walk the Line • I'm Yours • Imagine • Over the Rainbow • Peaceful Easy Feeling • The Rainbow Connection • Riptide • more.

00149250 ....$16.99

Also available:
00292082 **First 50 Melodies on Ukulele** ...$15.99
00289029 **First 50 Songs on Solo Ukulele**..$15.99
00347437 **First 50 Songs to Strum on Uke** .$16.99

40 Most Streamed Songs for Ukulele

40 top hits that sound great on uke! Includes: Despacito • Feel It Still • Girls like You • Happier • Havana • High Hopes • The Middle • Perfect • 7 Rings • Shallow • Shape of You • Something Just like This • Stay • Sucker • Sunflower • Sweet but Psycho • Thank U, Next • There's Nothing Holdin' Me Back • Without Me • and more!

00298113..............................$17.99

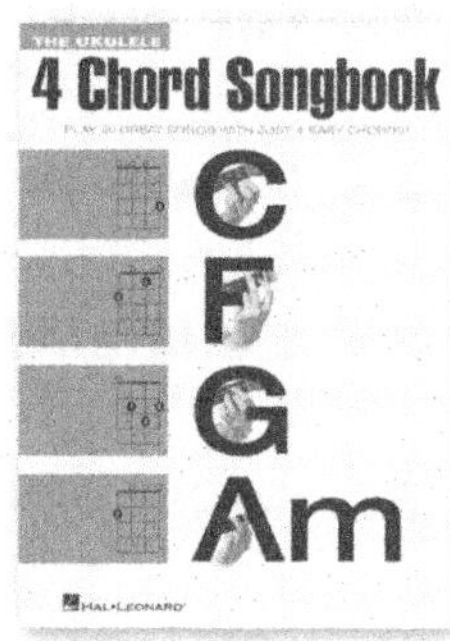

The 4 Chord Songbook

With just 4 chords, you can play 50 hot songs on your ukulele! Songs include: Brown Eyed Girl • Do Wah Diddy Diddy • Hey Ya! • Ho Hey • Jessie's Girl • Let It Be • One Love • Stand by Me • Toes • With or Without You • and many more.

00142050........$16.99

Also available:
00141143 **The 3-Chord Songbook**.........$16.99

Pop Songs for Kids

30 easy pop favorites for kids to play on uke, including: Brave • Can't Stop the Feeling! • Feel It Still • Fight Song • Happy • Havana • House of Gold • How Far I'll Go • Let It Go • Remember Me (Ernesto de la Cruz) • Rewrite the Stars • Roar • Shake It Off • Story of My Life • What Makes You Beautiful • and more.

00284415..............................$16.99

Simple Songs for Ukulele

50 favorites for standard G-C-E-A ukulele tuning, including: All Along the Watchtower • Can't Help Falling in Love • Don't Worry, Be Happy • Ho Hey • I'm Yours • King of the Road • Sweet Home Alabama • You Are My Sunshine • and more.

00156815........$14.99

Also available:
00276644 **More Simple Songs for Ukulele** .$14.99

Top Hits of 2020

18 uke-friendly tunes of 2020 are featured in this collection of melody, lyric and chord arrangements in standard G-C-E-A tuning. Includes: Adore You (Harry Styles) • Before You Go (Lewis Capaldi) • Cardigan (Taylor Swift) • Daisies (Katy Perry) • I Dare You (Kelly Clarkson) • Level of Concern (twenty one pilots) • No Time to Die (Billie Eilish) • Rain on Me (Lady Gaga feat. Ariana Grande) • Say So (Doja Cat) • and more.

00355553..............................$14.99

Also available:
00302274 **Top Hits of 2019** $14.99

Ukulele: The Most Requested Songs

Strum & Sing Series

Cherry Lane Music

Nearly 50 favorites all expertly arranged for ukulele! Includes: Bubbly • Build Me Up, Buttercup • Cecilia • Georgia on My Mind • Kokomo • L-O-V-E • Your Body Is a Wonderland • and more.

02501453..............................$14.99

The Ultimate Ukulele Fake Book

Uke enthusiasts will love this giant, spiral-bound collection of over 400 songs for uke! Includes: Crazy • Dancing Queen • Downtown • Fields of Gold • Happy • Hey Jude • 7 Years • Summertime • Thinking Out Loud • Thriller • Wagon Wheel • and more.

00175500 9" x 12" Edition $45.00
00319997 5.5" x 8.5" Edition $39.99

Order today from your favorite music retailer at
halleonard.com

Prices, contents and availability subject to change without notice